Education and
Neoliberal Globalization

Routledge Research in Education

Education and Neoliberal Globalization

Carlos Alberto Torres

Routledge
Taylor & Francis Group
New York   London

First published 2009
by Routledge
711 Third Ave, New York, NY 10017

Simultaneously published in the UK
by Routledge
2 Park Square, Milton Park, Abingdon, Oxon OX14 4RN

Routledge is an imprint of the Taylor & Francis Group, an informa business

First issued in paperback 2012

© 2009 Taylor & Francis

Typeset in Sabon by IBT Global.

Library of Congress Cataloging in Publication Data

Torres, Carlos Alberto.
  Education and neoliberal globalization / by Carlos Alberto Torres.
    p. cm. — (Routledge research in education)
  Includes bibliographical references and index.

  1. Education—Economic aspects.   2. Education—Social aspects.   3. Education and globalization.   4. Neoliberalism.   I. Title. II. Series.
  LC65.T67 2009
  306.43—dc22
  2008012614

ISBN13: 978-0-415-99118-6 (hbk)
ISBN13: 978-0-415-53671-4 (pbk)

Contents

Foreword

Pedro A. Noguera

Is it possible to oppose what Carlos Alberto Torres describes as neoliberal globalization? In these chapters, Torres argues with passion and great persuasiveness that it is not only possible, but absolutely necessary. Torres makes the case for opposition by making it clear that acquiescence to this steamroller of a trend and fatalistic acceptance of its consequences will contribute to human suffering and misery on a monumental scale.

The reader will undoubtedly find much of what Torres argues convincing; he is, after all, a gifted writer and an eloquent champion of the marginalized and dispossessed. Yet, it is important to acknowledge that much of what he argues runs counter to the discourse contained in the "news" and official information made available to readers and viewers throughout the world. According to the *New York Times*, the *Wall Street Journal*, Reuters, and all of the other "official" sources of news and information, neoliberal globalization, which might be interpreted crudely as the triumph of the market over human values, is much more than a trend or passing fad. Neoliberal globalization now constitutes the dominant worldview on matters pertaining to trade, finance, political economy, and even public education. Increasingly, neoliberal globalization is the new paradigm for rational thought, and those who stand in opposition to it run the risk of appearing, at the minimum, off-base, and at worst, insane.

Torres is not afraid of taking on powerful enemies or opposing trends that seem insurmountable. Fortunately, he is also not the only opponent of neoliberal globalization. As its effects have become more apparent and manifest in the form of rampant environmental degradation, hyperexploitation of workers in globalized sweatshops and assembly lines, and in the field of education, a narrow focus on testing with little regard to the role of education in supporting democracy and human liberation, the ranks of its critics have grown. In fact, no meeting of world leaders from wealthy nations is possible anymore unless extreme measures are taken to shield the political and economic elites from the legions of protesters who are invariably drawn to express their opposition to their global dominance. Yet, opposition—even if expressed in well-organized, angry protest—has thus far had little influence on neoliberal globalization. Despite the protests, its detractors cannot hope that it will eventually fade away as awareness of its negative side effects grows. Nor can they compare neoliberal globalization to some debilitating disease that will eventually pass once it has run its course. For Thomas Friedman, Lawrence Summers, the *Wall Street Journal,* and all the other progenitors of neoliberal globalization, it is the new reality, the new paradigm, the new system to which we must either adapt or perish.

In these essays, Carlos Alberto Torres makes it clear that he not only stands in opposition to the conventional wisdom as reported by the "experts" and all the newspapers and television stations controlled by Rupert Murdoch, he also does so in ways that can inspire others to do the same. His message is unequivocal: neoliberal globalization can be contested, challenged, and undermined by illuminating and exposing the moral weakness upon which it has been constructed. Such a call stands in stark contrast to the many voices of officialdom that contend that globalization is nothing more than the logical growth and extension of capitalism, which never was a purely national economic system, and is now truly a global system. For its cheerleaders, the emergence of neoliberal globalization will render the state and all its accoutrements (including public education) obsolete. Globalization makes it possible for market forces to transcend national boundaries for goods (drugs and guns particularly), ideas, music, disease, and people, and to move freely with little regard to the traditional barriers that once separated people and places—language, culture, currency, and sovereignty. As Thomas Friedman (2005) has argued, the world is increasingly flat, and with ongoing innovations in telecommunications, it is also getting smaller.

Torres makes it clear that the sunny picture created by the advocates of neoliberal globalization disguises the ugly effects it has upon the poor and powerless. He urges his readers to look beyond the rhetoric of politicians who, under the guise of *leaving no child behind,* do little to improve the conditions under which children live and learn, even as they hold up testing and accountability as the new panacea for a failed public education system. Like his mentor, Paulo Freire, Torres reminds the reader that the purpose of education must be to humanize the learner so that each individual can function as subjects capable of creating and shaping their own history, rather than passively accepting their positions as workers, soldiers, consumers, and victims on the world stage.

Torres writes:

> It is my hope that these essays of opposition, which reclaim the importance of theory to think about and grapple with these realities, are useful for those who fight in the first line of defense of identity, nationality, dignity and human rights.

In these pages, Torres offers ammunition for those ready to engage in the fight against neoliberal globalization. At a time when so much of the official word tells us otherwise, such a message is not only timely, but absolutely essential if indeed the creation of another world, one that is less unequal, less unjust, less unsafe, and less polluted, is possible.

Pedro Noguera

Introduction
Social Theory and Education— Against Neoliberal Globalization

"It is again necessary for me to upgrade my knowledge of the world which is ingenuous, spontaneous, alienated and alienating. So I accept the world as the object of my epistemological mind, of my critical research, my vigilant curiosity. 'Conscientization' is primarily an act of vigilance by which I enter, little by little, into the very essence of the facts in front of me as knowable objects so I can discover their quiddity."

—Paulo Freire[1]

The text that the reader has in his or her hands is composed of essays that have been written for different audiences and delivered in different places and different languages over the last five years, but until now have not been gathered together and published in English.

They represent a stage in my reading, investigation, analysis, and political struggle against one of the most perverse phenomena in contemporary culture and education: neoliberalism.

Neoliberal governments promote notions of open markets, free trade, the reduction of the public sector, the decrease of state intervention in the economy, and the deregulation of markets. A more detailed description, analysis, and criticism of neoliberalism, neoliberal governments, and the neoliberal state—terms that I use interchangeably—is provided throughout this book. One observation, however, is in order. As Michael Apple has stated in several of his own works, neoliberalism and neoconservativism are two sides of the same coin. While neoliberalism emphasizes the economic characteristics of a model of global capitalist hegemony, neoconservatism offers, as an addendum that is not contradictory to the above stated principles, a set of moral and ethical codes, which dovetail quite nicely with the principles of neoliberalism.

However, when it comes to some specific aspects of social policies (for instance, appointments of judges, questions of school segregation, right to choose policies, etc.), one may not overlook the differences. Yet, the overall policy tools, policy rationale, and strategy for the corporative rule of the planet remains, by and large, very similar. Likewise, it seems relevant to also argue that the shared consensus, certainly in the United States at least, among the power elite of how to protect and expand their privileges, makes these two models (like the two mainstream political parties in the United States) very compatible, and in some instances, completely indistinct in their values, policy orientation, and overall political project. Yet, once again, the devil is in the details. The historical struggles over social policy in the United States force choices, and not surprisingly, for many progressive communities, groups, social movements, and intellectuals, the logic of the lesser evil prevails in supporting policy choices and preferences.

AGAINST NEOLIBERALISM: THE LEGACY OF PAULO FREIRE

The public can now follow in English what was, for me, an important lesson in my last conversation with Paulo Freire. Although it may appear to be a nostalgic remembrance, I want to relate the experience that was, for me, enormously instructive.

At the end of April 1997, I was traveling to Madrid from Los Angeles, where I have lived for almost two decades, to participate in a conference organized by the Universidad Complutense and the University of California.

On the way to the airport I had a sudden impulse to call Paulo Freire. I cannot recall why I felt such urgency, but we had been planning to write a book together about new educational challenges at the threshold of the twenty-first century. The book had a tentative title: *The Possible Dream of Education.*

We wanted to update the discussion about some of Paulo's great theses and think about ways to implement them in classrooms of the advanced capitalist world. We wanted, to use a phrase dear to Paulo, to "reinvent and not to repeat Paulo Freire."

I called him from my cellular phone on the way to the airport. Paulo answered the phone in his house in São Paulo and, after the customary greetings, I told him that I was flying to Europe and wanted to know when and where we could meet to work on the book. He told me that he would be giving a course at Harvard that fall and perhaps it would be easier for me to travel to Cambridge to work with him. Cambridge would provide us a more tranquil workplace than São Paulo, without the enormous demands that the academic, political, and educational life of Brazil imposed on Paulo's agenda.

I asked him if he had been thinking about the overriding themes we would be addressing. His response was not only direct but seemed almost laconic: "Carlos, we have to criticize neoliberalism. It's the new demon of the world today." At that moment, there was a silence at the other end of the telephone that let me know that we had lost our connection. I was arriving at the Los Angeles International Airport, and the power of the communications systems in the area might have interfered with our call.

I hesitated to call him back. My boarding time was near and, of course, a cellular call is always costly. I decided to call him on my way back from Paris, where I would be working for a few days after the meeting in Madrid. I started to think about an academic meeting at the Catholic University of São Paulo with retired São Paulo Cardinal Paulo Evaristo Arns, who had been one of the foremost Brazilian representatives of the Theology of Liberation, along with Paulo Freire. The title of this meeting was "The Diabolic and the Symbolic," and it seemed to me a good one because, theologically speaking, the symbolic is the antithesis of the diabolic. The interrupted conversation with Freire stayed with me as I pondered the theme.

I never imagined that while I was in Paris, I would learn of Paulo's sudden death, on May 2, 1997, of a heart attack soon after an operation on his coronary arteries. Paulo died alone while he was recovering from the operation in the intensive care unit.

One of the great masters of Latin America, with his prophetic gestures, white beard, and eyes that reflected the dedicated authenticity of his utterances, captivating readers and listeners alike with his logic and his poetry, was dead. An enormous piece of the history of our cherished and conflictive continent died with him. Freire was one of the twentieth century's most important political philosophers of education.

I am convinced that *Pedagogy of the Oppressed* represents the most important contribution to the educational philosophy of the second half of the twentieth century, just as John Dewey's *Education and Democracy* marks the first. These now classic texts have shaped generations of educators and social militants all over the world. They are books full of key thoughts that continue to raise questions.

With Paulo Reglus Neves Freire died a thinker who changed the way we understand education, beginning with the publication of. *Education as the Practice of Freedom* and *Pedagogy of the Oppressed* inaugurated a politico-pedagogical agenda that grew stronger with successive publications, particularly his final book, *Pedagogia da Autonomia,* published forty days before his death, an important text about pedagogical ethics. It was a book that Freire wrote without a title, without any subheadings, just a manuscript that evolved around Freire's perceptions of the politics of ethics in teaching. Moacir Gadotti, Freire's closest friend and main biographer, received the manuscript from Freire's hand, read it cover to cover, and added, with Freire's consent, the subheadings and suggested the title, *Pedagogia da Autonomia,* (the title and subheadings that were altered in the English translation after Freire's death).[2]

As a thinker, Freire showed us that dialogue and deliberation are weapons in the fight to build education as a public sphere. Freire taught us like few others that education and politics are inseparable, and occasionally indistinguishable, in the social weft of the human adventure.

With epistemological rigor and his characteristic poetic sensitivity, he taught us that:

conscientization cannot be based on a consciousness isolated from the
world without creating a consciousness-world dialectic. Conscientization cannot be based on the belief that world transformation and world
creation take place within the consciousness, but rather that the process
of transformation occurs through praxis in the world itself, in history.[3]

I wrote these texts with Freire's last words to me resounding in my head.
Ours was an affective, working connection that lasted more than twenty
years, beginning with my first book about his work, in 1975, which included
many citations.[4]

These essays are in opposition to neoliberalism. In other words, they
oppose the arrogance of power, injustice, the lack of love in this world
where it seems that established power, especially that of the United States
of America, has decided to create a world system governed by an ethics of
permanent war instead of peace.

They are essays in opposition to the myths of neoliberal education. We
go back to Freire who stated thirty-five years ago that:

> . . . the day that the forces of power and domination which govern science
> and technology are able to discover a way to kill intentionality and the
> active character of consciousness which makes consciousness perceptible
> to itself, we will no longer be able to speak of liberation. But precisely
> because it is not possible to kill or blot out the creative, re-creative and
> receptive force of consciousness, what do those in command do? They
> mystify reality because, as there is no reality other than the reality of con-
> sciousness, when the reality of consciousness is mystified the conscious-
> ness of reality is mystified as well. And by mystifying the consciousness of
> reality, the process of the transformation of reality is obstructed.[5]

THE STRUCTURE OF THE BOOK

The book is divided into three parts. The first part provides a critique of
neoliberal globalization. Chapter 1 illustrates the terms of reference for
the analysis of neoliberal globalization as a specific model of globalization
and its impact on education. Chapter 2, using the example of the politics
of the World Bank, offers a systematic criticism of neoliberalism and its
pedagogical model. Chapter 3 analyzes and criticizes the foundations and
implementation of neoliberalism in the United States (the No Child Left
Behind Act enacted by the Bush administration).

The second part offers different alternatives to neoliberal globalization.
Chapter 4 offers an analysis of the role of teachers unions and its possibilities to develop an alternative leadership, while Chapter 5 discusses the
potential contributions of Paulo Freire's political pedagogy to challenge the
deleterious tendencies of neoliberalism. Chapter 6 offers a set of arguments
on the importance of critical social theory for educational research and

the role of critical intellectuals. Chapter 7 summarizes some of the critical issues in the context of transformative social justice learning, and offers a draft of a theory of marginality, which may prove crucial for the context of the struggle of progressive forces against neoliberal globalization.

The third part shows that biographies are a genre of political and pedagogical struggles for critical educators.

WHY THIS BOOK, AND WHY NOW?

We live in this world at a juncture where the development of global capitalism has shown that many of humanity's great achievements in human rights in recent centuries have begun to be eliminated. I refer to the fact that boys and girls ought to be in school and not working in factories as members of a cut-rate workforce, or that male and female workers ought to receive just and dignified wages, or that there ought to be racial and ethnic equality and not institutional mechanisms of discrimination, or that women's rights, obtained after long and difficult collective struggles, ought to be respected and preserved. This is only to mention a few of the social rights won by important social struggles that neoliberal globalization seems to try to erase from the face of the earth.

It is also a moment when cynicism seems to be the philosophy that animates the thinking of the middle class. Recently I spoke critically in a private meeting with a young woman employed in the entertainment industry in Los Angeles about the situation of young girls in Thailand, working for pennies for multinational companies like Nike. She replied that, by working in the factories, Thai children of both sexes avoided having to sell their bodies in the streets. As if enslaving young workers were the solution to the problems of poverty that led to the prostitution of boys and girls!

Frankly I began to wonder whether there has been real human progress in our struggle for an education that enlarges social rationality, equity, and equality, as well as justice and peace, as postulated with a certain naiveté to be sure, by the movement of the Enlightenment.

It is obvious that many of the great accomplishments of the Enlightenment and of liberalism, if they have not been totally wiped off the face of the earth, have been profoundly affected by neoliberalism. Freire was, again, premonitory:

> the process of conscientization that does not proceed through the revelation of reality to the organization of the practice of transforming the reality it sets out to know, is a process doomed to fail.[6]

I hope that these essays of opposition, which reclaim the importance of theory to think about reality, are useful for those who fight in the first line of defense of identity, nationality, dignity, and human rights. I refer to the teachers in our schools, teachers of adult education, the students,

professors, and researchers of higher education, the civil rights activists
and militants in anti-globalization movements, as well as intellectuals and
social action groups who posit the need for planetary consciousness as an
alternative to neoliberal globalization.[7]

With the passage of time and considering the brutality of the common sense
orchestrated by the mass media in the creation of the neoliberal hegemony
(the reader should not forget that I live in Los Angeles and have the rare privilege of experiencing the business of Hollywood *prima facie*), I have become
convinced that it is in the development of alternative communications media
and the work of school systems and universities that the fight for democracy,
multiculturalism, and citizenship will play the final card before the possible,
but not necessarily inevitable, social and cultural catastrophe of humanity.
Even from the margins of society we can construct a better future.

Paulo Freire was convinced that "conscientization as a manifestation of
utopia or as an instrument of this utopia has to be a task that implies an
ideological option on our part."[8]

The education as a possible dream, to which Paulo Freire invited us, is
today not only a demand but also, if I may say so in a Kantian spirit, a categorical imperative in the construction of a world where it is easier to love.

I want to end these first words by paying homage to Paulo Freire, critical
conscience of Latin America, as we remember his death 11 years ago with
a poem I wrote on the first anniversary of his death:

A little more than a year ago
(For Paulo Freire)

A little more than a year ago, your magic was still strolling these streets.
    Like a troubadour, you were singing songs of freedom.
The faces of children, youths, adults and old people were still practicing
    All possible vowel combinations: be bi ba, bo, bu.
Curiosity was, once again, the basis of epistemology
    And your generosity was challenging power.

A little more than a year ago, hope and wisdom still bore your name,
    And utopia too,
Amid rancorous outcries, rows and popular knowledge
    Wet with oppression but tempered
By amorous encounters of unknown intensities.
A little more than a year ago, your words were still shaping hymns,
    Destroying palaces, crumbling temples,
Inviting us to an immoderate revolution,
    And an impatiently patient struggle.

A little more than a year ago, Latin America was still full of
    contagious optimism,

Borders, barbed wire and bayonets were being erased
Like the indistinguishable characters of an extinct past while
Circuses, carnivals and processions were gathering, in their
splendor,
The legacy of tradition and rupture.
Men and women were looking to politics
For truth, justice and liberty.

A little more than a year ago, we still had you here, among us.
Today, in your infinitely suffocating death, you still live within us.
A little more than a year ago you ascended in a sonorous vocal choir
of words repeated
But reinvented as well,
Of traditional but not antiquated teaching,
Of prophecies where love is the fair measure of all things,
And where ethics and smiles are the banners and shields of an
ancestral battle,
Like your lessons, teacher, friend who continues among us.

Part I

A Critique of Neoliberal Globalization

1   Globalizations and Education[1]

A PORTRAIT OF CONTRASTS, CONTRADICTIONS, AND CONFLICTS

> Our civilization . . . is a civilization which has destroyed the simplicity
> and repose of life; replaced its contentment, its poetry, its soft romance
> dreams and vision with the money-fever, sordid ideals, vulgar ambi-
> tions, and the sleep which does not refresh.[2]

Last September, I was traveling by train from Porto to Lisbon, Portugal,
when I witnessed what struck me as a familiar scene in the lovely Portuguese
countryside. It was raining. A man left a shack, a very humble house, lit a
cigarette, and began to walk. A barking and quite aggressive dog tied to a
makeshift doghouse greeted him. The man kicked the dog in the jaw with
what seemed to me was formidable force. The apparently ferocious animal
quickly hid in the doghouse howling in pain. While the rapid passing of
the landscape through the windows of the first class wagon fragmented my
observations, like a slow motion frame-by-frame movie, I remember the
man, walking a few more meters and shepherding a dozen or so sheep that
were leisurely grazing not so far away from the doghouse.

I remember asking myself: Is this globalized Europe? That is, a Europe
full of animal rights activists, sophisticated capital lending, highly developed food technology, and extensive social movements challenging capitalism, globalization, and American imperialism? Or is this simply an example
of life in a third-world village, which happens to be located on the Iberian
Peninsula at the heart of the old continent?

Let me elaborate a bit on this impressionistic example, because it is tell-
ing of one of the principles of this chapter: globalization is a contradictory
phenomenon full of tensions and contradictions. To me, the man in the
shack was a shepherd tending to a small herd of sheep, perhaps not enough
to bring sufficient food to the table. The act of kicking the dog shows total
disrespect for an animal as an inferior being that easily can be sacrificed at
the mercy of our own temper. The simplicity of rural life accounts for contradictory phenomena as well; one that is well exemplified in Mark Twain's

epigraph that I used in the heading of this section. Yet, one may think that my example could be either a simple folksy episode or, on the contrary, a description of a scene that sharply reflects the complexities and contradictions of social life.

No matter what conclusion one may reach regarding the conflicts of knowledge management and behavior in the era of globalization, one may think that some of the precepts of the Enlightenment have faded away. Moreover, one may also conclude that if one places this example in the broader context of the post-September 11th world, the discussions on globalization, markets, knowledge, subjectivity, and education have been dramatically altered.

Globalization has been defined as "the intensification of worldwide social relations which link distant localities in such a way that local happenings are shaped by events occurring many miles away and vice versa."[3]

David Held suggests, among other things, that globalization is the product of the emergence of a global economy, an expansion of transnational linkages between economic units creating new forms of collective decision making, development of intergovernmental and quasi-supranational institutions, an intensification of transnational communications, and the creation of new regional and military orders. Considering the combining effects of education and globalization, there are at least two possible scenarios.

EDUCATION AND GLOBALIZATION:
TENTATIVE SCENARIOS

The first scenario is that globalization reflects, and eventually heightens, conflicts and contradictions of social life in the context of differential processes of internationalization of social relations deeply affecting (or, as in the case of my example, touching in rather limited fashion) portions of the globe. A second scenario will argue that, no matter what globalization has achieved, or what the pros and cons of globalization may be as a set of social relationships or an ideology, after the 11th of September 2001, the situation has been altered in terms of worldwide market dynamics and security concerns.

In the first scenario, a great deal of the arguments from the Enlightenment about the role of education in the process of internationalization of the world could be more easily applied. That is to say, education may help bring down barriers pushing for open markets while simultaneously training more competent workers to compete in those international markets.

For instance, the argument advanced by Robert Reich, an economist who was Secretary of Labor in the Clinton administration, is that the United States can no longer compete solely by means of cost-cutting because there are workers in other parts of the world willing to produce for lower salaries than their American counterparts. According to Reich, the comparative advantage of the United States lies in its ability to rely on highly qualified workers, with great flexibility, precision and specialization. Given that in the global economy new scientific discoveries and innovations are appropriated globally at a surprising velocity, and are implemented on standardized products, the only factor of production that is relatively immobile is labor. What counts at the level of the international workforce is its competitiveness, vision, and capacity to work collaboratively.

Reich distinguishes between types of workers or occupations in an internationalized economy. There are routine production service workers, in-person service workers, and symbolic–analytic service workers. The *routine production service worker* is the classic blue-collar worker of enterprises of massive, high-volume production. This also includes supervisors and white-collar workers that carry out monotonous activities. The *in-person service* workers realize simple and repetitive tasks, are paid in hourly wages, are intensively supervised, and generally do not require more than a high school education, except for occasional vocational training. The principal requirement of this group of workers is to be punctual, reliable, and courteous in dealing with the public. Finally, the *symbolic–analytic service workers* are those who work on the identification and solution of problems, including strategic mediation activities and brokering. Examples of this are scientists and researchers, design engineers, software engineers, financial consultants, tax consultants, specialized lawyers, organization specialists, public relations executives, film directors, producers, editors, production designers, investment bankers, real estate investors, etc. The majority of them have a university level education and, on occasion, a graduate degree.[4]

Reich's proposal is that only symbolic analysts contribute great value to the internationalized economy. One of the historical reasons for the high concentration of these workers in the United States is the link between industry, protected residential areas, and universities of an international category (e.g., Silicon Valley and Stanford University in California are classic examples of such a link). If Reich is right, a central concern for the development of public universities in Latin America and other developing countries should be—in addition to performing their traditional roles in science and technology, letters, and humanities—their ability to produce increasing numbers of symbolic analysts.

In contrast, the role of education in the second scenario becomes less clear. This is particularly true when the push for open markets loses supremacy to imperialist behavior leading to preemptive strikes. A manufactured war in the search for weapons of mass destruction, which have hardly been found, or potential nuclear instability in the Korean peninsula, are just a few international factors that deserve recognition given their currency and gravity.

These crises call into question the role and effectiveness of the State as a modernizer and social regulator. Paradoxically, during the seventies and eighties, the Left had been criticizing the ideological and repressive apparatus of the State. Since the nineties some business analysts like Keinichi' Ohmae denounce the nation-state as a creature of the past, arguing that the real centers of wealth creation are the region-states.[5]

For Ohmae, the four I's (that is, investment, industry, information technology, and individual consumers) drive the expansion and operation of the global economy, taken over the economic power once held by the nation-state. The result of this economic process is the rise of the region-state, defined simply as an area that often comprises communities situated across borders that develop around a regional economic center having a population of a few million to twenty million people.

From a neoliberal perspective, Ohmae offers a devastating critique of the nation-state, coupled with a critique of liberalism and democracy, because these are unable to satisfy popular demands while at the same time offering a minimum of public services. Ohmae's argument could be considered a right-wing perspective of what James O'Connor called in the seventies the "fiscal crisis of the state,"[6] or what has been termed in a famous Jürgen Habermas book, the dilemmas of legitimacy of the capitalist state.[7]

It is perhaps unnecessary to argue about the relevance of these questions for education, particularly when in the twentieth century, the educational systems and practices have been sustained, organized, regulated, and certified by the state. In fact, public education is a function of the state in terms of legal order or financial support. The specific requirements of certification for the basic teaching qualifications, textbooks, and curriculum are controlled by official agencies and defined by specific politics of the state."[8]

EDUCATION AND GLOBALIZATION: SOME HYPOTHESES

Multiple Globalizations: Tentative Scenarios

Let me propose the following hypothesis: there are multiple processes of globalization interacting simultaneously in a fairly convoluted fashion. Yet, all of them are deeply affected by the dynamics of international relations from the past few years, and by implication, they affect the role education and educational reform may play in the improvement of people's lives and societies. The idea of multiple globalizations deserves to be discussed in detail before we embark in a discussion about their educational impacts.

There is one layer of globalization, which I have called "globalization from above," in which an ideology of neoliberalism has called for the opening of borders, the creation of multiple regional markets, the viability of faster economic and financial exchanges, and even the presence of forms of state other than the nation-state, shrinking state services, and its overall presence in civil society. Selective deregulation is the motto of this globalization process.

There is a second layer of globalization representing the antithesis of the first, known as the "anti-globalizers," or what could be named "globalization from below." These are individuals, institutions, and social movements that have actively opposed what is perceived as the neoliberal globalization. For these social sectors, groups, individuals, and communities, no globalization without representation is their motto.

There is a third layer of globalization that pertains not so much to markets, but to rights: the globalization of human rights. With the growing ideology of human rights taking hold on the international system and international law, a number of traditional practices (from religious practices to esoteric practices) that have always been considered inherent to the fabric of a particular society or culture are now being called into question, challenged, forbidden, or even outlawed. Advancement of cosmopolitan democracies and plural citizenship is the motto of this globalization process.

There is also a fourth layer of globalization that goes beyond markets, and to some extent against human rights, that pertains to the globalization of the international war against terrorism. This new globalization has been prompted in full scale by the events of September 11th—which were interpreted as the globalization of the terrorist threat—and the reaction of the United States. The antiterrorist response has been military in nature, with two coalition wars led by the United States against Muslim regimes in Afghanistan and Iraq. Yet, the overall feeling of this process was not only its military flavor, but also its emphasis on security and control of borders, people, capital, and commodities—that is, the reverse of open markets and fast commodity exchanges. Security, as a precondition of freedom, is the motto of this antiterrorist globalization. Not surprisingly, its nemesis—terrorism based on religious fundamentalism—will endorse the motto that only chaos will bring about freedom.

Hence, globalization is a multiple and contradictory phenomenon, with deep-rooted historical causes, and, if one thinks of the tenets of human rights, for instance, a historical process that is difficult to reverse or even confront. Let us now explore in some detail these four possible layers of globalization *vis a vis* its educational implications.

The Educational Impact of the Multiple Layers of Globalization

The Neoliberal Globalization Agenda in Education

Agencies, multilateral or bilateral, such as the World Bank, the International Monetary Fund (IMF), and some agencies of the United Nations, including UNESCO and perhaps OECD, have promoted the model of neoliberal globalization. The hypothesis of Antonio Teodoro, following the work of Roger Dale and Boaventura de Souza Santos, is that there is a low-intensity globalization of education in Europe, with OECD being the architect of the process.

> The globally structured agenda is defined above all having as nerve center the great international statistics projects and, in particular, the INES project of the Center for Educational Research and Innovation (CERI) of the OECD.[9]

This agenda includes a drive toward privatization and decentralization of public education, a movement toward educational standards, and the testing of academic achievement to determine the quality of education at the level of students, schools, and teachers. Accountability is another key tenet of the model.

There has been a wave of educational reforms influenced by the globalization process under neoliberal inspiration. Martin Carnoy has classified these recent reforms in three types. The first type is reforms that respond to the evolution of the demand for better-qualified labor in the national and international labor markets; these reforms are based on new ideas of how to reorganize schools and improve the professional competence for a successful performance. Carnoy has classified these as "competition-based reforms." There is a second type of reform that responds to the restriction of budgets in the private and public sectors. These reforms are termed by Carnoy as "reforms based on financial imperatives." Finally, there is a group of reforms that try to improve the political role of education as a source of mobility and social equality. Carnoy has classified these reforms as "equity oriented reforms."[10]

The first type, or *competition-based reforms,* are characterized by four conventional strategies including: a drive toward decentralization of educational governance and administration of schools (e.g., a drive toward municipalization), new educational norms and standards that usually are measured through extensive testing (the new standards and accountability movement), introduction of new teaching and learning methods leading to the expectation of better performance at low cost (e.g., universalization of textbooks), and improvements in the selection and training of teachers.

The second type of reform, *based on financial imperatives,* is usually advocated by the IMF and the World Bank as a pre-condition to educational lending to the countries. These reforms also include a series of strategies. Among these are, first and foremost, the transference of educational financing from higher education to lower levels of education—under the premise that to subsidize higher education is to subsidize the rich, since the majority of the students enrolled in higher education are mostly from middle class and/or affluent families.

Discussing access to higher education in Argentina, a university professor argued that:

If you take 100 students at say first grade what you will find is that the number of people who finally make it to a university and graduate is less than four. So, there is very little access, because there is dramatic attrition at the very initial levels of the primary system. So the university is essentially an elitist university. Although not all of the people who are there are members of the elite. At best, it is a middle-class phenomenon. The poor do not make it to the university. The poor dessert the system and we can never recover them. [11]

The data for California high school graduation of people of color, which as an educational system is vastly better endowed in terms of financial resources than its Latin American counterpart, is only slightly better. For instance, Gary Orfield, Director of the Civil Rights Project, previously at Harvard University and currently at UCLA, and author of the book *Dropouts In America: Confronting the Graduation Rate Crisis,* argued that large urban school districts in California have become "dropout factories."[12]

An **education for all** was one of the key premises of the failed "Education for All Initiative" sponsored in Jomtien, Thailand, in 1990 by UNESCO, UN Development Program (UNDP), UNICEF, and the World Bank. The meeting attracted the participation of government representatives from 155 countries and more than 150 nongovernmental organizations who pledged to provide education for all by the year 2000. As the argument goes, investments in lower levels of education, namely primary and secondary education, will result in higher rates of return and a better equity–investment ratio than investments in higher education.

A second strategy is the privatization of elementary and secondary education with the notion that increasing user fees and family contributions to the education of their children diminishes, in turn, the fiscal pressure on financially strapped public sectors. Third, a cost-reduction strategy increases the number of students per professor as a way to cope with financial deficits[13] and growing student enrollments or both.[14]

The third major type of reform, *equity-based reforms,* seems to be simply a smokescreen, an add-on to the first two as their main legitimation. As Carnoy explains, the argument to transfer funds from higher education to lower levels of education is justified on the premise of investing for equity purposes. Similarly, equity policies attempt to serve and provide educational opportunities to women, girls, indigenous people, and rural populations—all of who are at a disadvantage in absolute and comparative terms with their counterparts, namely men, boys, and nonindigenous and urban populations. For instance, bilingual and multicultural programs destined to address the needs of linguistic minorities, special education programs, or out of school programs for disadvantaged and "at-risk" children, are all examples of equity focus reforms seeking quality of education for those sectors.

Carnoy concludes that equity-based reforms, given the dynamics of globalization, are postponed or are simply paid lip service by neoliberal governments and bilateral organizations:

> Globalization tends to distance the governments from the reforms based on equity for two reasons: first, it increases the relative payoff of high levels of qualification, limiting that complementarity between reforms oriented to competitivity and reforms oriented to equity; secondly, in the majority of the developing and in many of the developed countries, educational reforms, given the new economic global framework, are based essentially on financial imperatives, and tend to reinforce inequality in the educational supply.[15]

In closing this section, it is important to emphasize that privatization policies are crucial elements of the reforms oriented toward promoting open markets and, as such, they are important policy tools of neoliberalism. On the one hand, the pressure of fiscal spending is reduced by the privatization of public sector enterprises. On the other hand, privatization is also a powerful instrument for depoliticizing the regulatory practices of the state in the area of public policy. However, as it has been clear in the last two decades, the implications of growing privatization and the push for market policies limiting the state's role for subordinate social sectors are serious:

> In the context of the market forces, the state's interventionist role is likely to decline. This will have implications for all categories of people who, by virtue of their already weak position in spheres of knowledge, skills, access to goods and services and control over resources, need some protective legislations and provisions. Left to themselves in the open market, their situation is likely to get further deteriorated.[16]

Finally, privatization policies are preferred policy instruments even if the outcome of some of its instruments, as in the implementation of vouchers, is not at all clear. For instance, in August 2000, in the midst of the U.S. presidential debate, a Harvard Professor and vouchers advocate, Paul E. Peterson, released a study of voucher programs in New York, Dayton, Ohio, and Washington, D.C. His analysis based on randomized field trails showed that school vouchers significantly improved test scores of African-American students, while voucher results for other racial groups were not statistically significant. The work of Peterson and associates suddenly gained national prominence in terms of the politics of the presidential race—Bush supported vouchers while Gore opposed them. The finding that, after two years, a group of African-American students using vouchers to attend private schools scored six percentile points higher than their control groups in public schools quickly become news, and conservative editorial writers and columnists seized on the occasion to show how out of touch Gore was on pressing educational matters. The facts were clear and persuasive, according to voucher defenders. Yet three weeks after those findings were first reported, Mathematica, a Princeton-based research firm that had been a partner in the study, issued a sharp dissent, questioning the implications of the findings, considering them quite provisory, but it was already too late to impact public opinion.

Most recently, Alan Krueger, a Princeton economist having access to the full database made available in the public domain by Mathematica, reanalyzed the data, showing that the results reported came from only one of the five grades studied in New York. This was originally Mathematica's questioning of the findings released by Peterson. Moreover, reanalyzing the way race was defined in the original analysis of the data (including the race of the father rather than only of the mother); Krueger was able to expand the total sample size of African Americans from 519 to 811. Considering this new sample, vouchers appear to have made no difference for any group. Clearly, as Hank Levin has indicated years ago, data is a political prisoner of governments, and I might add, of political ideologies as well.

Globalization as Anti-Globalization: Evidence from Higher Education in Latin America

The movements of anti-globalization in favor of social justice and equality have had important dissident voices. The chorus of critics of the process of globalization advanced by the Group of Seven[17] in their meetings include the late Pope John Paul II and the Catholic Church, various Protestant Churches jointly with feminist movements, ecological and Greenpeace movements, environmental coalitions, indigenous rights groups, and communist, socialist, anarchist, and libertarian groups. In short, there are a vast and growing number of discontents with globalization.[18]

The rich array of worldwide anti-globalization views and actions have had obvious consequences for educational reforms and narratives. In this section, however, I will focus exclusively on the critiques of neoliberal globalization within higher education, drawing from my recent work in Latin American higher education.[19]

Latin America's public higher education institutions have a very distinguished and long tradition of academic work based on the notion of autonomy and financial autocracy.[20] Despite this tradition, for the last two decades these institutions have faced the hammering of the neoliberal agenda of privatization, decentralization, and accountability based on entrepreneurial models—including productivity incentives.[21] Our research focused on two distinct, large, and distinguished universities in the region, the National University of Mexico (UNAM) and the University of Buenos Aires (UBA).

Interviews with faculty members, administrators, scientists, and political leaders yielded contentious results. For instance, an Argentinean professor claimed that globalization is nothing but economic colonialism.[22] A major concern in our interviews in Mexico was the view that there was an imposition of US-based neoliberal models of higher education. Such imposition came as a result of structural adjustments to policies, as well as at the hands of Mexico's own leaders.

Accountability and incentives were also a contentious issue. A UNAM professor commented on Mexico's three programs designed to increase salaries: PRIDE, which offers a surplus for performance; the National System of Researchers, offering another surplus for performance in the form of minimum salaries added to researchers' income; and the salary from the university. He argued that:

> You can get 1/3 of our salary from the university, 1/3 from PRIDE, and 1/3 from the System of National Researchers. But you have to fill out tons of paper work just to earn a reasonable salary. With these three programs and the behaviors that they encourage, we start to resemble the professors in the U.S. However, there is a big difference. We have to sustain a very high level of performance simply to elevate our salary to a reasonable wage, whereas in the U.S. sustaining such high levels of productivity often results in elevating one's salary above the norm.[23]

In Argentina, the economic crisis and the need for university reform are seen as interrelated, but as a professor noted, her research team perceives that there is a strong tendency to see globalization as Americanization, believing that many of the transnational economic policies supposedly designed to open up world markets actually serve the interest of powerful policy makers, such as the United States.[24]

Issues of academic sociability and the sense of a university's social mission are being eroded by the neoliberal ideology and agenda. As a Mexican professor complained:

> It's [neoliberal globalization] destroying the collective identity that Mexican intellectuals have had in the past. So, it's changing the academic culture from one defined by a social collective, to a group of individuals acting for their own interest.[25]

Even one of the highest administrators of Latin American higher education sharply pointed out that:

> There is no national vision from a neoliberal perspective—there are only markets and the logic of markets dictate everything. And so, in Mexico, national culture, national identity, and the role of the national

university are all in transition. What will become of the university? Who knows? Can we generate a national project within an increasing neoliberal society?[26]

Globalization, Human Rights, and Education

While the questions posed above are hard to come by and to answer, the presence alone of the layer of globalization of human rights poses another round of issues to be addressed by educational institutions. The question of human rights in education has become a central question for citizenship and democracy, and indeed for education. Huhoglu Soysal's analysis of the limits of citizenship in the era of globalization highlights some of these issues. She argues that:

> . . . the logic of personhood supersedes the logic of national citizenship [and] individual rights and obligations, where were historically located in the nation state, have increasingly moved to an universalistic plane, transcending the boundaries of particular nation-states.[27]

Nuhoglo Soysal's analysis of the limits of citizenship has implications at three levels: First, at the level of citizenship, where notions of identity and rights are decoupled; second, at the level of the politics of identity and multiculturalism, where the emergence of membership in the policy "is multiple in the sense of spanning local, regional, and global identities, and which accommodates intersecting complexes of rights, duties and loyalties;"[28] and finally, given the importance of the international system for the attainment of democracy worldwide, Nuhogly Soysal highlights the emergence of what could be termed cosmopolitan democracies; that is, international political systems that are relatively separate in their origin and that constitute dynamics from the nation-states' codes."[29]

For instance, critical stances to human rights from feminist perspectives criticize the concept because "It's Western, it's male, it's individualistic, its emphasis has been on political and not economic rights."[30] Yet, despite these criticisms, "Human Rights are seen as . . . a powerful term that transforms the discussion from being about something that is a good idea to that which ought to be the birthright of every person."[31]

If the agenda for human rights is reconfiguring the boundaries of nations and individual rights of national citizens, and they are seen as a precondition to attain basic equality worldwide, the educational systems have to reflect, more and more, the tension between human rights as a globalized ideology of cosmopolitan democracies, and the growing nationalistic feeling in many educational systems that were built as powerful tools of the Enlightenment. This tension is also projected in questions of identity and the rights of cultural and religious values to be upheld independently of the ideology of human rights and its demands upon educational systems. This, of course, plays a major role in considering the role of education in the growing globalization of the world.

The Globalization of Terrorism and Antiterrorism: Some Educational Implications.[32]

The most obvious change in the last few years in the process of globalization is the terrorist attack of September, 11ᵗʰ 2001, which undermined the invincibility of the United States, never before attacked in its continental territories, and the implications of this attack for the global economy, politics, culture, and education. There is a heightened feeling that most salient among these transformations are the changes in the definition, enjoyment, and administration of freedom worldwide.

Nevertheless, we have not yet seen in the United States or elsewhere how these changes are provoking a new understanding of patriotism in the schools. In concluding his assessment of his personal feelings and his professional responsibility as a teacher in dealing with the September 11ᵗʰ attacks, cultural critic Michael Apple warns us of unintended, and perhaps still unobservable, consequences of the events:

> In any real situation there are multiple relations of power. Any serious understanding of the actual results of September 11 on education needs to widen its gaze beyond what we usually look for. As I have shown, in the aftermath of 9/11 the politicization of local school governance occurred in ways that were quite powerful. Yet, without an understanding of "'other' kinds of politics, in this case race, we would miss one of the most important results of the struggle over the meaning of 'freedom' in this site. September 11 has had even broader effects than we recognize.[33]

The reverberations of the attack and the ensuing global war against terrorism will have important consequences in an ever more interconnected global world, especially in education. For instance, a casualty of September 11ᵗʰ in the United States, and a factor that presumably could affect other industrialized countries given changes in visa requirements and process, is the availability of international education for foreign students—not a minor source of income for the countries involved. The United States is the biggest exporter of international education; there were

> 547,867 'foreign students' studying in American institutions in 2000/2001. This represents earnings of US$ billions to its national economy. . . . Trailing behind the United States, the 2ⁿᵈ largest producer of international education is the United Kingdom. In 1999/2000, the U.K. enrolled 277,000 international students of which 129,180 were university students. Earnings from the international education exports

and consumption of goods and services by students was estimated then at 8 billion British pounds."[34]

Michael Apple's remarks discussing the question of schooling and patriotism is a fitting conclusion for this section:

> No analysis of the effects of 9/11 on schools can go on without an understanding of the ways in which the global is dynamically linked to the local (. . .) Thus, I argue that educators—whether teaching a university class or participating in local school board decision making—must first recognize our own contradictory responses to the events of September 11. We must also understand that these responses, although partly understandable in the context of tragic events, may create dynamics that have long-lasting consequences. And many of these consequences may themselves undercut the very democracy we believe that we are upholding and defending. This more complicated political understanding may well be a first step in finding appropriate and socially critical pedagogic strategies to work within our classes and communities to interrupt the larger hegemonic projects—including the redefinition of democracy as "patriotic fervor"—that we will continue to face in the future.[35]

The question of human rights and patriotism affecting the life of U.S. civil society is important. The role of education in preserving a sense of unity in diversity in multicultural, multilingual, and multiethnic societies like the United States is central, particularly preserving the concepts of tolerance and solidarity, which articulate the values of the Enlightenment. The risk, however, is to dispense with basic notions of tolerance inherited from the Enlightenment and end up sponsoring a patriotic stance that create an 'us' versus 'them' mentality, and eventually a model of religious and educational intolerance.

In a very different venue, however, one of the key elements seen as generating a global terrorist model is some form of Islamic education and fundamentalist religious schools. For instance, Pakistan's madrassas are considered training grounds for radical fundamentalist Islamic militancy. Some of them, particularly those in Pakistan's northwestern tribal regions, seem to have produced a sizable number of militants who have joined Al-Qaida and the Taliban movement in neighboring Afghanistan. Muslim seminaries in India and Pakistan are suspected of being linked to the attack on the Hindu parliament on December 13th, 2001, by a group of Muslim fanatics, attacks on Hindu temples in India in 2002, and to religious riots and communal violence in Gujarat.[36] Not surprisingly, the reform of religious education of the madrassas of Malaysia, Indonesia, and Pakistan are considered priorities in the international fight against terrorism, and the control of domestic dissent in those states.

CONCLUSIONS

Globalization is seen as blurring national boundaries, shifting solidarities within and between nation-states, and deeply affecting the constitutions of national and interest-group identities. What is new is not so much its form as its scale. Since the Breton Woods conference in 1944, in which the IMF and the World Bank were founded, national trade barriers have been eroded, and global economic forces have played a more significant role in local economies. In the six decades that followed that event, international trade has expanded approximately twelve times and foreign direct investment has expanded at two or three times the rate of trade investment.[37]

Some analysts have argued that we are witnessing the corporativization of the world, rather than simply its globalization.[38] Likewise, Octavio Ianni has suggested that there is a difference between globalization as a historical process, which cannot be reversed, and the question of globalism, a process articulated by neoliberalism and coordinated by global corporations.[39] Yet, those leaders confronted by the anti-globalization movement seem to have less control over the world economy than some analysts assumed they have. The European Union is an example of how national borders are being blurred by economic realities.

As my introductory example seems to indicate, with a shepherd kicking a dog as I was comfortably relaxing in a first class train seat, the postmodern cultures of transportation, technology, and mass media are being confronted by local traditional communities, and by the new movements exercised by cosmopolitan communities based on programs of human rights. Yet, as Bosnia, Darfur, and many African and Middle Eastern situations indicate, human rights are also confronted by the programmatics of ethnic nationalism.

Insofar as education is concerned, this chapter has attempted to show that there are multiple layers of globalization, all of them impacting education differentially, though in convoluted yet interrelated forms. The agenda of neoliberal globalization has been systematically analyzed, criticized, and challenged by progressive forces worldwide. Yet it remains a formidable agenda in education, impacting developing and developed countries alike. The anti-globalizers have scored some public victories that have created an ethos of critique and utopia in the mass media.

One may argue that anti-globalization movements are part and parcel of cultures of activism but have not yet fully connected to larger social struggles at the local level. As Saltzman argues considering feminist debates and struggles:

> Cultures of activism . . . are collective expressions of oppositional behavior, thought, symbols, and action that arise as groups of individuals seek societal or institutional change in specific settings . . . [they]

may be connected to larger social struggles but are not synonymous with them.[40]

However, beyond declarations and political mobilization responding to actions of perceived globalizing institutions, the anti-globalizers have not yet produced sufficient critical mass of alternatives to be tested. In education, however, the four World Educational Forums held in Porto Alegre, Rio Grande do Sur, Brazil, appear emblematic, confronting jointly with the Social Forum the premises of the Davos Forum and the idea that neoliberal globalization is unstoppable. The following World Social Forum, which attracted more than a 100,000 participants from dissenting groups, took place in 2004 in India, while the World Educational Forum was held in 2005 in São Paulo by the Paulo Freire Institute, the municipality of São Paulo, and a large number of sponsoring institutions, attracting more than 100,000 educators registered as participants. This meeting was probably the largest educational forum that ever took place in the western world.

The presence of human rights, while emblematic of the prevalence of western ideology at the planetary level, are of course challenged by traditions and cultural as well as religious practices that have roots other than in the premises of the Enlightenment. This, of course, has implications at several levels of citizenship, democracy, and educational reform.

Debates about human rights and educational tolerance will be heightened by the globalization of terrorism as a universal threat and the coordinated reaction of, particularly, the United States and its allies in a movement that has emerged as the globalization of anti-terrorism.

Despite formally being an international effort, this globalization reflects the politics of unilateralism put forward by the Bush administration as their foreign policy doctrine, and hence placing the United States at odds with international public opinion and the foreign policy of the major economic powers in the world, particularly France and Germany, but most recently with growing opposition from Russia, Italy, and Spain, including a critique from Amnesty International.

Under the title "War on Terror" Human Rights Issues," unilateralism is treated by Amnesty International as a doctrine that undermines international law. This is what Amnesty International published in September 2006:

At the United Nations General Assembly, President Bush recently spoke of "broken treaties," UN resolutions being "unilaterally subverted," and of the United States' wish for the UN to be "effective, and respected, and successful." Yet, in the two years preceding this statement, the US government has increasingly dismissed or rejected multilateral treaties. The US Government

* has undermined the UN Charter by threatening preemptive, unilateral military action in Iraq.

* continues to reject provisions of the Geneva Conventions that pertain to the treatment of prisoners detained at the US Navy base in Guantanamo, Cuba, and in other regions of the world.

* has withdrawn its signature from the treaty establishing the International Criminal Court and launched a worldwide campaign undermine the Court's jurisdiction.

* stands virtually alone in the world in its failure to ratify the Convention on the Rights of the Child and other human rights treaties.

* continues to sentence child offenders to death despite the fact that this practice is prohibited by human rights treaties and has been virtually abolished outside of the United States.

Such actions weaken the framework for international peace and human rights that the United States was a leader in establishing after World War II. They threaten to undermine the value of US commitments and they risk alienating allies at a time when international cooperation is crucial. They also send a message that it is acceptable for governments to ignore their obligations under international law.[41]

The implications of unilateralism, the Patriotic Act, and the Bush Administration's war against terrorism, for the United States as a polity, and for education in the country, are very serious. The conundrum is how to avoid a form of patriotism that may undermine human rights and traditional liberalism. Similarly, how to be sure that the secular insularity of the United States, despite its façade of liberalism and international stances, will not be reinforced by a conservative government-sponsored ideology of patriotism and by new-born Christians who are ready to throw the baby out with the bath water.

In international terms, the debate has focused on the extent that the U.S.-sponsored wars against Afghanistan and Iraq, and the more recent support of the United States of the 2006 Israeli attack on Lebanon, is not destabilizing the globe even more, creating more rancor and grievance against the United States and western societies, and providing breeding grounds for Islamic fundamentalist extremism.

Perhaps it is appropriate to end this analysis of the connections between globalizations and education with a suggestive statement by Paulo Freire:

Maybe we have enjoyed our present democratic freedom so much that we are passionately dreaming about it. However, this taste and this passion for freedom coexist with authoritarian traditions and practices, resulting in one of our ambiguities.[42]

2 The Banking Education of the World Bank

Expert Knowledge, External Assistance, and Educational Reform in the Age of Neoliberalism— A Critique of the World Bank[1]

INTRODUCTION

This chapter discusses the implications of expert knowledge in educational reform in the Third World, with an emphasis on the moral imperatives of external aid and expert knowledge.

Expertise is usually associated with formal training (education), including achieving a fair amount of experience in a given field. The notion of expert knowledge has been developed in cognitive psychology encompassing three different components: formal knowledge, practical knowledge, and self-regulating knowledge.[2] Päivi Tynjälä synthesizes these areas in the following way:

> Formal knowledge belongs to the category of what cognitive psychologists have called declarative knowledge. Such explicit and factual knowledge has played a mayor role in education, and as such it constitutes the core of professional competence. The second constituent of expertise, practical knowledge, often called procedural knowledge, manifests itself as skills or "knowing how" while formal knowledge may be described as universal and explicit, practical knowledge is, rather, personal and tacit, being thus intuition-like and difficult to be expressed explicitly. The third component, self-regulating knowledge, consists of meta-cognitive and reflective skills that individuals use to monitor and evaluate their actions.[3]

Our discussion of expert knowledge takes as a case in point the dominant theoretical paradigm, role, policies, and practices of the World Bank, pointing to the risks and liabilities involved in external aid and expertise in educational reform. Nonetheless, because of its brevity and its particular goal, this chapter cannot be understood as an extensive and systematic criticism of the World Bank and/or it's experts, nor is it a systematic criticism of positivism as a theoretical paradigm informing the expert knowledge of the

World Bank, or the institutions of capitalist regulations in the world *per se*. The goal of this chapter is to highlight some of the key themes of the expert knowledge of neoliberalism, as represented in the work of the World Bank, and to emphasize the role that positivistic models of teaching, learning, and research play in the process.

The World Bank has the rare privilege of being criticized by representatives of the Right and Left. Hence, there is abundant critical bibliography that could be used to illustrate the implications of World Bank's expert knowledge and policy orientations.

For instance, from a conservative perspective—the same perspective that seems to underscore the viewpoint of key sectors in the US Republican Party—it is argued under the suggestive title "The Dismal Legacy and False Promise of Multilateral Aid" that

> Multilateral lending institutions—the International Monetary Fund (IMF), World Bank, and regional development banks—have flooded the Third World with hundreds of billions of dollars in aid. Since the early 1950s, the World Bank alone has lent developing countries nearly 300 billion. Those institutions have also played a major role in encouraging Western governments to provide hundreds of billions of dollars more in bilateral assistance to the developing world. Yet after providing advice, loans, and grants to the governments of the world's poorest countries for four decades, the multilaterals can point to few, if any, cases in which their efforts have led to improved standards and sustained economic prosperity. Instead of growth, the Third World has experienced social disintegration, economic stagnation, debt crises, and, in some regions, declines in agricultural production and incomes (p. 1).[4]

From the other intellectual corner of the street, one may find, for instance, the incisive criticism of John Harriss to the notion embraced by the World Bank in their prevailing discourse on development that to attain social capital is the 'missing link' in development. Harriss claims that the recent focus on the World Bank rhetoric to promote social capital, as

> norms of generalized reciprocity and networks of civic engagement give rise to social capital, which in turn makes cooperation between people possible, and reinforces reciprocity and civic engagement.[5]

For Harriss, the notion of social capital developed by the World Bank is simply a ruse to depoliticize the discussion on development. Moreover, as an analytical concept, social capital, the keystone in the new development strategy of the World Bank, is devoid of any meaningful content. By evading issues of context and power it only helps to decontextualize and depoliticize the question:

Even careful studies that attempt to measure the effects of social capital are unsatisfactory because "social capital" remains a statistical artifact, and the questions of what causes what, and by what mechanisms or social processes, remain unanswered.[6]

Despite my own interest in epistemology, I make few references throughout this chapter to the World Bank's prevailing notion of positivist rational choice perspective, with its social theory built from a model of individual behavior assuming that: "Actors have a single principle of action, that of acting so as to maximize their realization of interests."[7] This premise, prevalent in most World Bank documents, is worthy of serious epistemological debate, a task obviously beyond the objectives and scope of this chapter.

I focus on expert knowledge in the era of neoliberalism. Neoliberalism, or the neoliberal state, are terms employed to designate a new type of state that emerged in Latin America and many other areas of the world in the last three decades. The first example of economic neoliberalism in Latin America is usually associated with the policies implemented in Chile after 1973. In many respects, neoliberal policies are in support of free trade and small public sectors, and against excessive state interventionism and tight regulation of markets. Lomnitz and Melnick, among other scholars, argue that, historically and philosophically, neoliberalism has been associated with structural adjustment programs. Structural adjustment, in turn, is usually described as a broad range of policies recommended by the World Bank, the International Monetary Fund and other financial organizations.[8] Although the World Bank differentiates among stabilization, structural adjustment, and adjustment policies, it acknowledges that the general use of these terms "is often imprecise and inconsistent."[9]

However, I do not want to simply add another voice to the chorus of critiques of the World Bank. I want to discuss some of the practical alternatives to expert knowledge employed by regulatory institutions of capitalism, presenting some of the moral imperatives and ethical challenges in educational reform, the focus of my concluding remarks.[10]

Finally, while I have decided, given the necessary brevity of this chapter, not to extensively discuss the notions of neoliberalism or globalization,[11] a central premise of my analysis is that globalization processes influence Third-World educational reform in different ways. Yet, neoliberal globalization is not wholly hegemonic, pervasive, all-encompassing, or uncontested at the local and global level. Likewise, while I insist that, in terms of policy orientations, the age we are now living is the age of neoliberalism, it does not, as any hegemonic model, go uncontested, nor has it demonstrated itself to be technically and, more importantly, politically, capable of ruling with an 'iron fist' that cannot be challenged or defeated. As the election of Luiz Inácio Lula da Silva , who replaced the experience of the neoliberal government of Fernando Henrique Cardoso in Brazil, shows, neoliberalism may lose legitimacy and the power to govern.[12]

The Logic of the World Bank: Neoliberalism in Education

It is important to begin by defining the role of the World Bank, in the context of international capitalism, as a regulatory agency of capitalism. This is important because as a bank, it is a lending agency, not a donor agency. The distinction between a lending agency and a donor agency is not necessarily made in the bibliography about international development and cooperation agencies. Since its creation in 1946, the World Bank "was a conservative institution that primarily funded infrastructure and other basic investments in less developed countries."[13] Since 1968, when Robert McNamara became bank President, it has been interested in promoting economic growth through capital investment.[14] Educational investment is not the most important investment area of the World Bank, especially in comparison with, for example, investment in infrastructure.

A second aspect of the lending policy of the World Bank and its expert knowledge approach is that it is proactive, not reactive. That is, the World Bank quite often initiates contact with countries to design specific loans—contacts that reflect the link between knowledge and expertise on the one hand, and finance lending on the other. Both aspects are inseparable from the general financing premises of the World Bank. Another element that must be taken into account is that the business of banks is to lend capital and receive interest on the loan—interest that is usually commercial, with few exceptions. The difference between these loans and commercial bank loans are that they are guaranteed by countries. Furthermore, the work of the World Bank is closely tied to the International Monetary Fund (IMF); without the endorsement of the IMF, it is not possible to enter into negotiations with the Bank. This is important because various economists and social scientists have spoken about the "Washington Consensus" as one of the forces that imposes the logic of structural adjustment in the world.[15]

The analytical premises of the World Bank can be categorized as supply-side economics.[16] Two elements radically affect the formulation of public policy: privatization and the reduction of public spending. These two policies are highly compatible, and in fact, privatization can be considered an important strategy for achieving reductions in public spending.

The privatization policies require additional explanation. These policies are crucial elements of the reforms oriented toward promoting markets and, as such, they are important policy tools of neoliberalism. On the one hand, the pressure of fiscal spending is reduced by the privatization of public sector enterprises. On the other, privatization is also a powerful instrument for depoliticizing the regulatory practices of the state in the area of public policy formation. That is, privatization plays a pivotal role in the neoconservative and neoliberal models because

> purchase of service contracting is both an administrative mechanism
> for addressing the particular issues of the social legitimacy of the

state involved in direct social services and an attempt to borrow from the managerial ethos of private enterprise and, (entrepreneurial development), systems of cost-benefit analysis and management by objectives.[17]

Neoliberals and neoconservatives have argued that the state and the market are two social systems that are diametrically opposed and that both are considered as real options for providing specific services.[18] Why then does there appear to be a preference for the market over the state? Neoliberals and neoconservatives consider that markets are more versatile and efficient than the bureaucratic structures of the state for numerous reasons. Markets respond more rapidly to technological changes and social demand than the state. Markets are seen as more efficient and cost-effective than the public sector in the provision of services. Finally, market competition will produce more accountability for social investments than bureaucratic policies.[19]

In addition to these policy preferences that George Soros and others have termed *market fundamentalism* is the fact that neoliberal thinking ties the privatization of public enterprises to the solution of the external debt problem. After all, in certain versions of the neoliberal ideology in economics, state enterprises were

> responsible for creating the Latin American external debt problem and, more importantly . . . their privatization may help resolve that problem.[20]

It is important to point out that the process of privatization is not free from conflicts and contradictions. For example, Ramamurty suggests that,

> it is by no means certain that substantial efficiency gains will be realized in the long run by privatizing large state owned enterprises with high market power.[21]

A second source of conflict has to do with regulatory mechanisms:

> Given Latin America's poor record of government regulation and the lack of established procedures and behind-the-scenes negotiations, it is difficult to be optimistic about the quality of regulation after privatization. Governments may renationalize some of these industries in the future, by choice or by necessity. If that were to happen, foreigners might have to be compensated for their investments at rates much higher than those received at the time of privatization, thus creating a potential large outflow in the future. Such conflicts could also damage relations with private investors, causing a recurrence of outward capital flight, at worst.[22]

A final comment about the philosophy of privatization is that many of its proponents postulate an anti-statist perspective rather than a privatization perspective. In other words, the question is whether they attempt to generate true competition in the market. Many of the models of privatization of state enterprises replace the monopoly of a state enterprise in a specific area with a similar monopoly by private enterprises.

In terms of specific educational policies, the World Bank has promoted policies of democratization of schooling, supporting the education of women and girls (in the best of the liberal–democratic tradition), basic education, and the quality of education. At the Jomtien Conference in Thailand, a number of international organizations, with the World Bank as the central architect supported by UNICEF, UNESCO, and UNDP, devised the model of "Education for All," a model in which the World Bank ideology played a major role, linking education for all to economic efficiency.[23]

A similar concern is expressed by Argentine economist, José Luis Coraggio, when he points out that since the World Bank is primarily composed of economists and not educators, the final objective is economic efficiency, freeing markets, and the globalization of capital—all of which lead to an overemphasis on quantitative methods of measuring the success of a policy. Using strictly economic criteria (for example, rates of return based on personal income), it is suggested by World Bank publications that an additional year of primary education in the lower levels produces larger increments in income than at higher levels of the educational system. Thus, if it is concluded that investment in basic or primary education leads to better results in terms of increasing gross national product, the problem, suggests Coraggio, is that the net increase in national product assumes that the principal resource of the country is a reservoir of flexible and "cheap" yet qualified workers who can produce goods and services for export. The real increase in income will be made not by those productive workers but by the consumers of those goods and services located in the industrialized world.[24] A similar concern was expressed a decade ago during analysis of the premises postulated in the preparatory documents for the Jomtien Conference and the serious implications for higher education policies in Latin America.[25] However, intellectual reasoning and ideology, while influential in designing policy, may not be sufficient to implement specific reforms.

The logic of instrumental rationality, which is pervasive in the documents of the World Bank and like-minded international and bilateral institutions, may not be sufficient to alter the almost impenetrable political rationality of governments (at national, provincial, and even municipal levels).

Conflict and contradictions in policy reform, and more importantly in the allocation of resources, plagued the attempt to create the educational alliances advocated for at the Jomtien Conference, and the great failure virtually everywhere of the much-heralded Education for All reform, demonstrates that even the most powerful players in the global educational system may not alter the intractable domestic realities and political alliances of the countries of the world.

However, it would be very naïve to imagine that the work of the World Bank and international lending and donor organizations are merely technical contributions, and that the specific political components of policies are left to the work of the country and political organisms. There is a strong political component to the World Bank. Its work began during the Cold War, and its directorate was, and continues to be, dominated by representatives of the United States and subject, to a large extent, to the politics of American diplomacy. Historically, the World Bank has reflected the threats (real or perceived) by the government of the United States on the part of its politically adversary ideologies and the wishes of the business community of the United States.[26]

Since its inception, the World Bank has given priority to specific educational policies, including, in a relatively chronological order, the construction of schools, support to secondary education, vocational and technical education, non-formal education, and more recently, basic education[27] and educational quality (defined in terms of rates of return and performance indicators). Some of the indicators that the experts of the World Bank have designed to measure the quality of education include spending per student, instructional materials (textbooks), the length of the school year and of the school day, and the social class of the teacher.[28]

The importance of the World Bank in promoting research and educational reforms worldwide meets specifications such as those of the Jomtien Conference proposals, and as such, the peculiar nature of external intervention masked under notions of external assistance and aid need to be revisited from ethical, political, and pragmatic perspectives. The next section presents a synthetic assessment and relevant questions and queries in trying to construct alternatives to neoliberalism in education.

Is it Possible to Think of Practical Alternatives to Neoliberal Interventions?

The complexity of many of the dimensions involved in the interaction between neoliberal international organizations, neoliberal governments, and local communities in the Third World should invite us to consider a multifarious set of questions. What follows is a preliminary and obviously incomplete checklist, which may prove useful for a democratic conversation about educational reform based on democracy and participation.

Is the Transnationalization of Knowledge a Problem for Third-World Countries? Revisiting the Financial–Intellectual Complex

Joel Samoff, one of the most astute and informed New Left critics of neoliberal educational policies has defined the World Bank as a leading component of a financial–intellectual complex, which pursues the transnationalization of knowledge and expertise using a community of experts for hire, in a process where there is a strong confluence of research and educational financing. This financial–intellectual complex has a pivotal role in the worldwide network of power and decision-making in education. Given its position in research and financing, the work and experts of the World Bank influence the international discourse. The Bank commissions long-term research and influences the selection and legitimizing of research topics (for example, educational quality and textbooks), the operational definition of the variables, the dominant terminology (for example, school wastage or student drop out which is an attempt to shift the blame onto the individual rather than thinking that many students are 'pushed out' of the system), and the analytical proposals and hypotheses, which are considered useful and reasonable for investment and educational development.[29]

Are Huge Salary Differentials a Problem for Democratic Accountability?

One central aspect of the functioning of the World Bank, and presumably of the majority of international financial organizations, is the overwhelming cynicism that makes moral and ethical questions occupy a secondary place when the high salaries of international and local experts are at stake. For example, the rumor in 1991 in Mozambique—ranked that year by the World Bank as the poorest country in the world—was that while the average annual salary of a worker in the country was $80, some local consultants to the World Bank were charging up to $8,000 a month for their services. This rumor about how much a local consultant to the World Bank earns could be, and probably was, incorrect. Nonetheless, whatever analysis of costs and salaries one might employ, they would demonstrate that the consultants of international organizations receive salaries totally incommensurate with the salary scales of developing countries. Facing dramatic economic determinants given the business cycle and natural/economic endowments of Third-World countries, moral and ethical questions can give rise to cynicism as a mechanism for dealing with reality.[30]

Do Mainstream Theories Play a Neocolonial Role?

Another central element to think about is the acceptable theories of educational planning—for example, Human Capital Theory—which are still mainstays of international organizations. One of the questions that has preoccupied researchers is whether neoliberal organizations such as the World Bank reflect the results of empirical evidence or the theoretical and operational preferences of the organization in their research. David Plank suggests that the theoretical preferences of the Bank led it to the following: 1) increasing investment in primary education and primary health care based on the argument that the rates of return for primary education exceed those of other levels of education; 2) administrative decentralization, with the understanding that the locally administered programs are more cost-effective than centralized ones;

3) investment in general education instead of investing in vocational education based on empirical evidence that general education is more productive in the long-run; and 4) recuperation of investment costs and efficiency in the management of resources. Plank concludes that these four principles appear to enjoy a life of their own, independent of the empirical evidence on which they are ostensibly based.[31]

If this were the case, then the instrumental reasoning of the World Bank, and of most, if not all, international financial organizations, would be playing a neocolonial role. This is especially true when educational policies are directed not so much toward improving the use value of the work force as they are toward improving the exchange value. Stabilization policies, fiscal conditions, and the economic drive toward export-oriented policies appear as policy preferences that are relatively homogeneously applied worldwide without virtually any concern for context-bound conditions. They appear as legitimate measures in the context of the internationalization and globalization of capitalism, and particularly, as totally compatible with notions of normal science and planning, i.e., positivism as the dominant thinking in international organizations.

Is Positivism Fault-Proof?

There is a strong positivistic component in the social sciences guiding educational planning in the regulatory institutions of capitalism. Therefore, it should be no surprise that the logic that predominates in these institutions is the logic of instrumental rationality. In positivism, the means are determined by pre-established ends and policy recommendations, which respond to the interplay of forces in a country, region, or specific municipality—after all, corruption is seen as the prevailing ethos of these countries not seen as quite democratic. Moreover, any attempt to take into account the historical and structural transformations of the past are ignored. In short, it is not surprising that, armed with positivism as the bedrock for their conceptual knowledge and instrumental rationality as their goal, most of the World Bank's policy recommendations ignore, by and large, the context-bound conditions and the histories that created local conditions and specificities. Is it, then, that the technical components are always rational and doable and yet always encounter a set of political circumstances that conspire against the process of implementation of those recommendations? So, is the problem in the political circumstances surrounding educational reforms in the Third World or, conversely, are there serious problems at the epistemic heart of the model on which these recommendations are generally based?

Samoff, among others, points to the different options, given that positivism is the predominant scientific paradigm in educational planning.[32] Numerous analyses of education can be carried out without necessarily relying on positivism, including feminism, postmodernism, critical theory, cultural studies, or Neo-Marxism. It is important to humbly accept the limitations of knowledge in historical–social sciences and the partial and conditional character of discoveries. It is necessary to reject notions of knowledge, which are built simply on a growing accumulation of facts, and to strive for a perception of the world characterized by discontinuities and small results with gradual consequences. After all, the transformations of knowledge in humanities and social sciences reflect the *historicity* of the subjects, as representatives of Existentialist philosophy noted many decades ago.

Another disputable aspect is the notion of ownership of knowledge, which results from research being commissioned and subsidized by organizations (national and international) that retain control over the results. Undoubtedly there are methodological options to mobilize knowledge in communities, such as participatory research or action–research—action, which offer a practical alternative to positivism, and are particularly useful for enhancing the degree of participation of the 'studied' populations in policy and planning. Numerous research projects based on dialectical perspectives and on methodological pluralism are options very different from the methodological monism of positivism. Finally, it is important to accept and protect criticism in academia as a way of confronting the authoritarianism of certain positivist perspectives.

Is Constructivism an Epistemological and Ethical Alternative to Positivism?

The polar opposite to positivism is a constructivist model of social science, which reflects a strong alternative vision in which reality appears as a product of discontinuities and unpredictable effects. Learners in the view of constructivists actively participate in learning, a notion that applies to the most elementary forms of learning and the most advanced forms of research. Paulo Freire and Lev Vigotsky come to mind here. Viewing all knowledge and learning as a social activity does not necessarily mean, as some postmodernists argue, that we cannot potentially represent reality, but it does imply that we must acknowledge the diversity of perspectives involved in the formation of a community, and a community of inquirers and teachers in particular. Abandoning the "quest for certainty" does not require abandoning the search for knowledge.

Methodological pluralism follows from a constructivist conception of scientific knowledge. This does not mean so much that anything goes, but rather that we must acknowledge that there are diverse logics in use that make up inquiry. Accordingly, the key issue for policy research is the development of coherent research designs that link theory and research techniques appropriate to the questions asked and problems to be solved.

A third premise, in stark contrast to positivism, is that knowledge cannot be separate from meaning and value. Thus, two implications are key here. First, we cannot imagine a social science devoid of social interest, and therefore, we cannot so easily dissociate the conceptual from the normative principles. Second, since, in the end, it is all about values and meaning, education is necessarily a moral enterprise. However, in a culturally diverse society, this does not imply an absolute moral code, as opposed to procedural principles for guiding ethical thinking and action. In the context of education, an ethic of caring, social justice, and individual responsibility are central principles of moral action that should complement each other.

As feminist theorists have reminded us, the nurturing principle of caring is at the heart of all learning as an interactive process that must respect the dignity of others. In the context of male-dominated cultures, an ethic of caring can emerge only through a feminist approach providing the foundations for change. Feminist scholars have argued that the male experience is overwhelmingly reflected in education, and more generally, in public policy. We need to take the culture of 'otherness' very seriously, specifically women's culture(s) and the cultures of minorities in schools, by broadening the perspectives of citizenship education to include responsible and mutually respectful behavior in the domestic unit, the family, and in interpersonal relationships in society at large. I am not here arguing for the need to 'stir in' some concerns for gender and women's issues to make social science more humane. Rather, I am arguing for taking the notion of standpoint theory very seriously, even with all its pitfalls and deficiencies, and to argue that without essentializing a given experience, gender counts as an important epistemological principle. Furthermore, as Nancy Hartsock has cleverly argued in defense of a feminist standpoint theory, this approach

> indicates a recognition of the power realities operative in a community, and points to the ways the ruling group's vision may be both perverse and made real by means of that group's power to define the terms for the community as a whole.[33]

In addition, Kantian principles of social justice provide rational grounds for justifying criticism of social relations that undermine caring and the equitable fulfillment of human needs. Lastly, a notion of individual responsibility is central to the constitution of morality and ethics in education.

Learning is also an interactive process that should be organized around dialogical principles. Though not necessarily undermining the importance of intellectual authority and leadership, dialogical principles as predicated by John Dewey and Paulo Freire, among others, do pose the question of the education of the educators and researchers and the need for reflexivity about what is to be taught and what the social uses of research are.

Finally, constructivists recognize that research and education are socially and historically situated activities in institutions that are constrained and enabled by the power relations in the society around them. For this reason, an understanding of the role of expert knowledge, research, and education should be considered from the political sociology of education, paying attention to the relationships of the ideals and values embodied in researchers and research practices that seek to inform and guide educational policies.

Can Third-World Governments Avoid the World Bank and Similar International Organizations?

Many educational policy-makers confronting the philosophy of privatization see this as a panacea for adjusting education to the market. Is it preferable or even possible to avoid interactions with the World Bank? In circumstances in which educational reforms of great magnitude are being considered, the World Bank, as a proactive institution, always seems to arrive offering its services, its analytical models, and its loans. This is true even in the case of a socialist political party such as the Workers' Party, or PT, in Brazil. In 1990, the PT won the municipal elections in São Paulo, and between 1990 and 1992 it developed an innovative educational policy directed by the radical educator Paulo Reglus Neves Freire. The World Bank sent a mission to São Paulo to convince Freire to accept financing from the Bank to carry out his curriculum reform projects and teacher training.[34] Freire, in a personal conversation with me, confided that he felt indignation about the World Bank experts' suggestions, and during a meeting he suggested that the mission return to the United States, and when they were in a position to solve the problems of education in the United States, they could return and speak with him about the situation in São Paulo. After this meeting, Freire explicitly communicated to the mayor of São Paulo, Luiza Erundina, that he would resign from his position if the World Bank's loans were accepted. Freire maintained his position, and during the educational administration of the PT in São Paulo, no World Bank loan was negotiated.

Obviously, the questions of whether World Bank loans should be accepted or if governments should deal with the World Bank regarding educational issues cannot be responded to in the abstract. Still, there are crucial questions that must be incorporated into the analysis of the neoliberal policies proposed by the World Bank. The first is related to the topic of democracy and accountability; that is, who responds to a government democratically elected and how countries should relate to international experts whose legitimacy is not determined through elections and who have any allegiance to the countries involved. This issue is central and it must be reiterated continually in the discussions about accountability. Some of the ideas of Herbert Marcuse from 1970s are useful to this critique, such as the fetishism of technology, the one-dimensionality and positivism (or positivization) of politics, and what Marcuse referred to as the *negative reason* via the depoliticizing of reason.

How About the Legality of International Lending?

There are different levels of legality regarding the acquisition of resources for educational investment depending on the administrative level (federal, state, municipal) being dealt with. In reality, most, if not all, loans that are obtained through negotiations with international organizations are guaranteed by the country, and thus, policies (and loans) may be negotiated by one government while another government is held accountable for repaying it. This is extremely dangerous, especially when the same problem arises within the international organizations; the experts of the World Bank are not accountable to countries but to the organizations that they represent. They are not even accountable in the sense that their research results do not seem to be the most important factor in the planning process; the signing of the loan by the Board of Directors of the World Bank is the overriding factor. Evaluation of the impact of the loan, whether its goals have been reached, the cost-effectiveness of the project, and of the implementation by the national responsible party are not extremely relevant once the loans have been guaranteed by the country, approved by the World Bank, and signed by the country.

Is Risk-Sharing Lending an Alternative?

It is increasingly necessary to think about a new international order that includes alternatives for dealing with agreements between countries and international institutions like the World Bank. One alternative would be the sharing of risks associated with investment, subject to the evaluation of a third independent party of the rationality *ex-ante* and *ex-post factum* of a loan, its results, and the working of the technical and operational teams of the World Bank and the national executing agency. Another alternative would be to create a pool of resources from the interest paid on loans that could be reinvested in multilateral organizations that would pressure the increase of loans for investment in social projects with interest rates, which are substantially lower than market rates. The interest on loans given to these projects would not be paid to the World Bank, but returned to countries for reinvestment in social programs to fight poverty and possible health epidemics (for example AIDS, cholera, bubonic plague) that are facing many countries as they enter the twenty-first century. A final element would be to stress lending in areas with extremely low economic rates of return (e.g., poverty-fighting programs) but extremely high social rates of return in terms of preventing political instability, child survival, women's needs, etc.

Educational Planning: Can Local Think Tanks Increase Local Control?

Another question involves thinking of planning mechanisms for education that do not necessarily follow positivistic logic and that are theoretically robust. This idea would be based on national organizations or 'think tanks' that could design alternative models of educational research and policy-making with democratic control at the local level (municipal, state, national/federal) and with technical competency and independence.

Aspects that are certainly more easily found in the more highly developed countries in the regions than in poor countries subject to 'brain-drain.' Salaries for these researchers and policy-makers would be competitive with local, regional, and international ones. These Think-Tanks would create new strategies for development that would be different from those prescribed by the neoliberal international organizations.

It is necessary that these think tanks have a permanent location, independent endowments, that they create new mechanisms of implementation and exert democratic control of projects. They must also have the technical capability (in terms of technical quality and also international management) and the political possibilities to engage in dialogue and negotiate with a wide range of institutions (including technical teams from international institutions such as the World Bank). The risk is obviously that they might become co-opted by political parties, and therefore may not remain independent, acting somewhat above the fray of institutional politics. Yet without a group of highly trained professionals who are relatively independent, well paid, and with new ideas that go beyond positivistic thought, it is impossible to imagine and design alternatives to the neoliberal models, which are beginning to show, especially in their practical application, the weaknesses of their theoretical formulations.

In closing, let me look at the moral imperatives and ethical challenges in external assistance and democratic educational reform in the Third World.

External Assistance, Moral Imperatives, and Ethical Challenges in Educational Reform: *A Guise de Conclusion*

I am aware that the challenges outlined below pertain to the overall interaction between external assistance and local knowledge/control of policy and not specifically to challenges of educational reform. That is to say, these are generic challenges to external interventions which apply, *pari pasu*, to the social role of research *per se*, with numerous implications for democratic educational reforms. However, because democratic politics are built on participation and representation, the nature, style, aim, and impact of external intervention in research, policy, planning, financing, or aid will determine the nature and operation of educational systems, educational reform, and perhaps even the destiny of the democratic discourse and the democratic conversation. The banking education heralded by the World Bank will never be the appropriate cognitive and political resource for citizenship and democratic politics.

Challenge One: The Gaze of the Anthropologist and the Authenticity of Local Communities. Dilemmas of External Assistance

Anthropologists have asked themselves, "Why study cultures we don't belong to?" "What are the ethics implied in this study?" "Who will benefit from the study?" "And how can an 'external' source of knowledge understand 'internal' sources of knowledge?" The problems of the gaze of the anthropologist are first whether he or she should be looking at the authenticity of local communities, and second, whether his or her gaze may penetrate the patina of reality and, in fact, reach out to understand that local knowledge. In other words, can the anthropologist know the authenticity of the community, preserving both the ethics of the profession and the ethics of the community? And in trying to know this community, can its authenticity be preserved once the knowledge of it has been accomplished? On parallel lines, these questions should be asked of people involved in external assistance, adding, perhaps, whether they have ever been confronted by the ethical dilemmas of (many) anthropologists, and whether they are prepared to consider the gaze of the anthropologist and the authenticity of the local community as part of their own expert work in the context of the globalization of capitalism.

Challenge Two: Science as Power

If we consider a perspective on science close to Foucault's view, science will be part and parcel of disciplinary forms of power. Its strategic aim is to increase social productivity and utility. The attempt to

> remake and re-conceptualize the world on the model of laboratory micro-worlds is neither a fully coherent project deliberately imposed from above nor an irresistible force that cannot be countered from below by those it affects.[35]

Thus, a dialectical view of science as power sees science, power, and resistance as naturally interlinked. This is an invitation to researchers to take ethical positions and to consider two-way relationships (e.g., external assistance/research and local communities), three-way relationships (e.g., external assistance/research, local communities, bureaucratic legal domination), and the degree of contradictions and ethics involved in each of these interactions. Who profits, who pays, who benefits from science as power should be perennial questions for people and institutions involved in external assistance.

Challenge Three: The Epistemology of Feminism and the Constitution of the Other

Does 'the other' exist *per se*, independent of 'us' or it is socially constructed? If the notion of the other is socially constructed, to what extent does the ability of constructing the other rest on notions of generalization and universality that are deeply marked by a masculine perspective. Constructivism has struggled for a long time to deal with the implications of constructing the other, and the epistemological criticisms of feminism to notions of universality should invite researchers to be extremely cautious, and, particularly, all-inclusive in looking at pedagogical discourses, needs assessment, and particularly the simplistic distinctions of who are 'we' and 'the other.' The constructivist perspective, outlined above, has been struggling with this issue for long time, and is able to offer a legacy of understanding and ways of seeing that are very compelling when compared to positivism.

Challenge Four: Freedom is Still to be Conquered

Freire's contribution to understanding education as the act of freedom is an invitation to see the interminable dialectics in the struggle to free ourselves and to free others from constraints to freedom. In and of itself, the struggle for liberation is another form of intervention that can be considered part of the ethics of intervention. Certainly, education as the act of freedom implies a different perspective on local, socially constructed, and generationally transmitted knowledge. It also implies a perspective that challenges normal science and non-participatory planning, constructing a theoretical and methodological perspective that is always suspicious of any scientific relationship as concealing relationships of domination. At the same time, while freedom is still to be conquered, freedom can be conquered because unequal, exploitative relationships are built by human beings and can be changed by human beings.

In short, these four challenges, which are by no means exhaustive of all the moral challenges involved in social research, show that research always moves between moral imperatives, ethical choices, and immoral realities. Researchers cannot avoid this fact, although we can deceive ourselves by adopting a cynical perspective and thinking that we only propose technical solutions, while others should take the difficult political and ethical decisions. It is not that easy.

3 No Child Left Behind
A Brainchild of Neoliberalism and American Politics[1]

INTRODUCTION: EDUCATION AND NEOLIBERALISM

> Neo-liberalism and neo-conservatism are in the driver's seat right now and this is not only happening in education.
>
> —Michael Apple, 2003: X.

Cultural critic and educator, Michael Apple, offers a critique of the current situation in education, in which liberalism has been displaced with neoliberalism, deeply affecting education and social policies:

> ... liberalism itself is under concerted attack from the right, from the coalition of neo-conservatives,'economic modernizers," and new right groups who have sought to build a new consensus around their own principles. Following a strategy best called "authoritarian populism," this coalition has combined a "free market ethic' with a populist politics. The results have been a partial dismantling of social democratic policies that largely benefited working people, people of color, and women (these groups are obviously not mutually exclusive), the building of a closer relationship between government and the capitalist economy, and attempts to curtail liberties that had been gained in the past. (Apple, 2004, p.xxiv).

Throughout the world, a neoliberal agenda is promoted by international organizations and some professional organizations of educators and researchers. In the case of the United States, this agenda is promoted by the American establishment, and includes a drive toward privatization and decentralization of public forms of education, a movement toward educational standards, a strong emphasis on testing, and a focus on accountability. That is to say, educational neoliberal reforms are based on an economic model of educational policy.

In this chapter, I define the No Child Left Behind Act (NCLB) as a neoliberal educational reform readily supported by the American establishment, and, as demonstrated in the 2004 presidential candidates' debates, the two mainstream parties hardly differ in their proposal for educational reform. Next, I will try to show how the NCLB affects educational practices, policies, and institutions, including higher education. Finally, I will offer a number of critiques of the NCLB from the perspective of social justice education.

THE NCLB AS THE EDUCATIONAL PANACEA OF THE AMERICAN ESTABLISHMENT?

> The economic model of education policy assumes a substantial consensus for a common set of educational goals. Unfortunately, such agreement rarely exists in the construction of real world reform.[2]

Any astute observer of the third presidential candidates' debate, which focused on domestic issues, will agree that the NCLB was never a matter of policy dispute between the candidates of the two mainstream parties. The challenger, Senator Kerry, did not question the values, implementation, effectiveness, or methods of the NCLB. Quite the contrary, he emphasized that:

> . . . the No Child Left Behind Act is really a jobs act when you think about it. The No Child Left Behind Act says, "We'll raise standards. We'll increase federal spending. But in return for extra spending, we now want people to measure . . . whether or not a child can read or write or add and subtract."

In the same vein, during the vice presidential candidates debate at Case Western Reserve University, in Cleveland, Ohio, Vice President Cheney said:

> I think the most important thing we can do is have a first-class public school system . . . And the president, his first legislative priority was the No Child Left Behind Act. It was the first piece of legislation we introduced. We got it passed that first summer on a bipartisan basis. And it does several things. It establishes high standards. It, at the same time, sets up a system of testing with respect to our school system, so we can establish accountability to parents and make certain that they understand how well their students are doing. And they have the opportunity to move students out of poorly performing schools to good schools. It's also important, as we go forward in the next term, we want to be able to take what we've done for elementary education and move it into the secondary education. It's working. We've seen reports now of a reduction in the achievement gap between majority students and minority students. We're making significant progress.

Thus the first important lesson is that the NCLB passed with overwhelming bipartisan support and enthusiasm because it reflects the perspective of the American establishment and the support of a number of professional organizations of educators and researchers.

Make no mistake: The NCLB increased the role of the federal government in accountability like never before. Although the federal government only funds 7% of the total expenditure of education in the country, it has tried to leverage those funds for specific purposes. De Bray explains the process:

> The 1994 ESEA reauthorization altered the federal role in account-ability for states and schools in two significant ways. First, the Clinton administration proposed that states adopt clear standards and assess-ments for all students in Title I, a strategy that was intended to use the money in Title I to drive the 'seed money' for standards-based reform provided in Goals 2000, a much smaller federal program enacted ear-lier in 1994.[3]

The NCLB creates a condition whereby the federal government dimin-ished the educational autonomy of the states strengthening the federal role by increasing requirements for states. The NCLB is a reform model that claims to raise standards while simultaneously defining what those stan-dards are, and what the quality of education is or ought to be. It is a model that bases the understanding of education in strictly and overwhelming eco-nomic terms (e.g., Senator Kerry's idea that the NCLB is a jobs act). It is a model based on cognitive measurements of students, schools, and teachers, making testing and accountability the buzzwords of the moment in educa-tional environments. And finally, as in the Wizard of Oz, "education" has become the magic word that is supposed to transform the world around us.

Listening to the President of the United States in the third presidential candidates debate at Arizona State University, I thought that President Bush was running for the Presidency of the teachers union, not for the Presidency of the United States. His answers to most of the pressing issues of the domestic policy agenda were 'education.'

- Do you want to keep the economy growing and maintain a competi-tive workforce? Education is the answer.
- Have you lost your job? Get an education.
- You need trade adjustment assistance? Go to community colleges.

This is the voice of President Bush during the third debate:

> I went to Washington to solve problems, and I saw a problem in the public education system in America. They were just shuffling too many kids through the system, year after year, grade after grade, without learning the basics. And so we said: Let's raise the standards. We're spending more money, but let's raise the standards and measure early and solve problems now, before it's too late. Got four more years, I've

got more to do to continue to raise standards, to continue to reward teachers and school districts that are working, to emphasize math and science in the classrooms, to continue to expand Pell Grants to make sure that people have an opportunity to start their career with a college diploma. And so the person you talked to, I say, here's some help, here's some trade adjustment assistance money for you to go a community college in your neighborhood, a community college which is providing the skills necessary to fill the jobs of the 21st century.

Senator Kerry concurs. During the second presidential candidates debate on October 8, 2004, at Washington University in St. Louis, Missouri, he argued:

I think you ought to get the break. I want to lower your cost to health care. I want to fully fund education, No Child Left Behind, special-needs education. And that's how we're going to be more competitive, by making sure our kids are graduating from school and college.

While agreeing with the President on the need for the NCLB, he blames the administration for underfunding it: "The president reneged on his promise to fund No Child Left Behind." This seems to be the cornerstone of disagreements between both parties—the appropriate level of funding for a substantial reform like this one. De Bray has argued that this is what undermined the consensus:

President Bush's budget for 2004 calls for significantly less education spending than what Congress has authorized. Further, as governors have slashed state education budgets, it is clear that states no longer have the capacity to implement the kinds of policies they did during the economic boom of the 1990s. If the federal government does not adequately fund the law's mandates, both Republican and Democratic governors will resist politically, as Vermont's Howard Dean (D) and Louisiana's Mike Foster (R) at different times suggested they might.[4]

Another slight difference between the candidates is that the key educational problem for Sen. Kerry, as he expressed in the second debate, is his emphasis on fostering global educational competition: "China and India are graduating more graduates in technology and science than we are." One may wonder, however, if such competition has to do with training a workforce or with different factors, such as the capacity of research and development in the United States to produce new knowledge and technology. Everybody knows that the United States' higher education system has been brain-draining other nations' human capital for decades, and that once students graduate, many simply remain working for American corporations. This may not be the norm any longer:

Testimony to this is the beginning of a 'reverse brain drain" manifested by a sustained drop in the number of doctoral students from China, India and Taiwan (China) who planned to remain in the United States beginning in the late 1990s.[5]

Thus the issue of international competitiveness in science and technology doesn't seem to reside solely in the national capacity to attract and/or educate scientists, engineers, and technologists, but perhaps in the creative productivity of such a work force:

"... Japan, the Republic of Korea and Taiwan (China) account for more than one quarter of all applications for industrial patents awarded in the United States each year and, remarkably, Taiwan (China) and Singapore surpassed the United States in the overall number of citations to their patents on chemical design."[6]

Still, while one may agree or disagree that the Unites States is lagging behind in science and technology compared to other nations, it is somewhat understandable why the issue of fully funding NCLB educational reform becomes the cornerstone of disagreements between Democrats and Republicans:

On the first anniversary of the signing of the No Child Left Behind Act in January, Democrats, including senators Edward M. Kennedy (D-MA) and Joseph I. Lieberman (D-CT), sent President Bush a letter that read in part, 'America's public schools cannot overcome the enormous obstacles they face on the cheap.' Their letter demanded a $7.7-billion increase in the federal education budget for the next fiscal year (2004). Bush, by contrast, has proposed a $1.1-billion increase, saying that the country cannot afford more in time of war.[7]

THE NEOLIBERAL GLOBALIZATION AGENDA AND HIGHER EDUCATION

Text and discourse are never innocent of complicity with events.[8]

Why do the Presidential debates usually take place at universities? Perhaps because they are considered sacred environments for the pursuit of the quest for knowledge, liberty, and freedom of thought, or perhaps because universities are seen as environments that welcome debate, as environments in which objectivity, neutrality, and apoliticism seem to prevail. This is not the place to discuss these common sense perspectives on universities, and in fact, it doesn't matter because the debates, as the one between President Bush and Sen. Kerry in 2004, were highly scripted, with little if anything left to the actual theoretical imagination or the methodological and analytical rigor of academic exchanges. The presidential debates were just 'spectacle democracy,' not actual intellectually and politically informed democratic exchanges.

As for higher education, neoliberal globalization designs four primary reforms for universities related to efficiency and accountability, accreditation and universalization, international competitiveness, and privatization.[9]

Concerns about efficiency and accountability are manifested in the efforts of legislatures, governing boards, and policy makers to increase the productivity of faculty while decreasing university and college expenditures. The classic example is the effort to increase faculty teaching loads without raising salaries. The proliferation of large classes in which one professor can reach hundreds of students is another example, as were early efforts to promote distance and Internet-based education. With regard to accreditation and universalization, major efforts are underway throughout the world to reform academic programs through accreditation processes and various strategies that produce increased homogeneity across national boundaries.

Reforms associated with international competitiveness are characterized by efforts to create measurable performance standards through extensive standardized testing (the new standards and accountability movement), introduction of new teaching and learning methods leading to the expectation of better performance at low cost (e.g., universalization of textbooks), and improvements in the selection and training of teachers. Competition-based reforms in higher education tend to adopt a vocational orientation and reflect the point of view that colleges and universities exist largely to serve the economic well being of a society.

Privatization, of course, is the final major reform effort linked to neoliberal globalization and perhaps the most dominant aspect. Neoliberal economic supporters view the marketplace as the ideal regulator of services, products, and costs. Consequently, if we think of education as a product or service, then from a neoliberal perspective the best way to regulate schools, colleges, and universities is to allow the market to do so. Nation-states need not fund or concern themselves with tuition costs; the market can take on such responsibilities quite handily. If institutions price themselves too high, prospective students will inform them by selecting other less costly institutions.

Alternatively, if a prospective student cannot afford higher education, then there are other options that societies offer, including military service and work within the service sector of the economy. The rationale of such a system is purely economic. Furthermore, the system is, from the perspective of neoliberalism, entirely just, given that subjective individuals do not open and close doors, but a system of costs and payments dictates nearly every outcome.

The neoliberal promise in education in the United States is one that points to progressively extending the model of NCLB to secondary schools, and eventually to universities, which is compatible with the most recent initiative of the World Trade Organization (WTO). The WTO, a multilateral agency heavily supported by the United States, has recently debated an initiative that promotes or attempts to ensure that educational services worldwide be deregulated and, on behalf of free markets, treated as any other financial service. This initiative opens the way for substantial higher educational reforms, to occur through privatization not only in the rest of the world, but also in the United States, a signatory of the WTO agreements.

PITFALLS AND CONTRADICTIONS OF THE NEOLIBERAL PROMISE IN EDUCATION

Maybe their meanness killed something important in them.[10]

From a perspective of teaching for social justice, a critique of the NCLB points to fundamental pitfalls and contradictions of the model that, in the end, not only may lead to its own demise, but will deeply damage the fabric of public education as the cornerstone of the democratic pact in the United States, and by implication, will damage peoples and entire communities, especially people of color.

Carlos Ovando offered eleven reasons why the NCLB could be considered a fraud in an oral presentation at the California Association of Freirean Educators (CAFÉ) organized by the Paulo Freire Institute-UCLA, on February 28, 2004. These reasons were originally developed by Stan Karp, author of the "The No Child left Behind Hoax"[11]:

1. The massive increase in testing that the NCLB will impose on schools will hurt their educational performance, not improve it.
2. The funding for the NCLB does not come anywhere near the levels that would be needed to reach even the narrow and dubious goals of producing 100% passing rates on state tests for all students by 2014.
3. The mandate that the NCLB imposes on schools to eliminate inequality in test scores among all students within 12 years is a mandate that is placed on no other social institution and reflects the hypocrisy of the law.
4. The sanctions that the NCLB impose on schools that don't meet its test score targets will hurt poor schools and poor communities most.
5. The transfer and choice provision will peak chaos and produce greater inequality within the public system without increasing the capacity of the receiving schools to deliver better educational services.
6. These same transfer and choice provisions will not give low-income parents any more control over school bureaucracies than food stamps give them over the supermarkets.
7. These provisions about using scientifically based instructional practices are neither scientifically valid nor educationally sound and will harmfully impact classrooms in what may be the single most important instructional area, the teaching of reading;

8. the supplemental tutorial provisions of the NCLB will channel public funds to private companies for ideological and political reasons, and as has been pointed out in debates about vouchers, not sound educational ones (Levin & Belfield, 2004).
9. The NCLB is part of a larger political and ideological effort to privatize social programs, reduce the public sector, and ultimately replace local control of institutions like schools with marketplace reforms that substitute commercial relations between customers for democratic relations between citizens.
10. The NCLB moves control over curriculum and instructional issues away from teachers, classrooms, schools, and local districts—where it should be—and puts it in the hands of state and federal educational bureaucracies and politicians. It represents the single biggest assault on local control of schools in the history of federal education policy.
11. The NCLB includes provisions that try to push prayer, military recruiters, and homophobia into schools while pushing multiculturalism, teacher innovation, and creative curriculum reform out.[12]

Karp and Ovando's critique is shared by many scholars, and there are also many other voices of dissent in many school districts and state departments of education struggling to comply with the letter and the spirit of the law. Yet, I will argue that even the spirit of the law, which is based on the notion of accountability, should be carefully inspected and criticized.

Technocrats and bureaucrats take for granted that accountability is one of those terms that cannot be challenged because it refers to the process of holding actors responsible for their actions. Nonetheless,

> Operationalizing such an open-ended concept is fraught with complications, starting with the politically and technically contested issue of assessing performance. Even if the measurement problem were solved, the factors explaining the process have received remarkably little research attention. For example, although political science has sought broad generalizations to explain wars, treaties, military coups, legislation, electoral behavior, and transitions to democracy, it has not produced empirically grounded conceptual frameworks that can explain how public accountability is constructed across diverse institutions.[13]

If a discipline such as political science has not been able to truly define what accountability is, how can one expect to sort out those dilemmas in education? Only in the feverish imagination of technocrats who, paraphrasing Mark Twain's irony, can be criticized for seeing all problems like nails because the only tool that they have is a hammer. I wonder sometimes what Rousseau, Pestalozzi, Dewey, or Freire, to name just a few great pedagogues, would say if confronted with the theories of the lesser-known pedagogues of Congress, the White House, and their academic advisers and consultants who inspired the principles of the NCLB.

Technocrats will probably argue that the rules of 'realpolitik' call for an understanding of systemic issues and the need of solving pressing institutional needs, and what is needed are practical solutions, hopefully through consensus, which cannot easily be made compatible with the lofty ideas of pedagogues. I will disagree. While recognizing the importance of those practical needs, the logic underpinning the rationales for policy formation, or the legal constraints of policy-making and institutional negotiation, there is no reason to base all policy on economic rationality, ignoring centuries of humanistic education, pedagogical research, or alternative models and critical perspectives. Or perhaps one simply may ask why a reform like the NCLB ignores vast amounts of contemporary scientific research that shows the difficulties of implementing its measures, and the pitfalls and dangers of those measures if implemented.

The complexities of the NCLB call for a more reflexive and critical understanding of contemporary schooling in the United States. While criticizing social reproduction, critical educators have been struggling to promote equity and equality in schools, alongside achieving good-quality education. To this extent, critical educators believe that better research findings, more consistent policy, better school management, teacher training, curriculum and instruction theories, and textbooks make a difference. Thus, to critically examine the foundations, instruments, methods, and policy orientation of the NCLB and its implementation makes a lot of pedagogical and political sense. Yet, there are other pressing questions of a greater order that we cannot ignore.

Even if the NCLB were to succeed in its implementation and premises, what difference do better schools—as defined by the NCLB—make for the betterment of our society if the overall orientation of the US government is to achieve global hegemony through the use of brutal force (disguised through new military euphemisms such as "smarts bombs"), and particularly acting as a world policeman in neoimperialist fashion, exporting democracy through carpet bombing in Iraq?

What difference do schools make in the training of children and youth who, eventually, will become the Centurions of the new Century? What difference do schools make in the education of people of color if they will become "green card Marines" in the imperial army? What difference do schools make in promoting social mobility if there are no jobs for the graduates after most of the best jobs have been outsourced out of the local markets and into a globalized market, benefiting the surplus value of globalized corporations? What difference do schools make in promoting multicultural traditions if, as many scholars have argued, there is only one dominant, hegemonic culture in capitalism, and that is the commodification of labor and knowledge and the culture of class?[14] What difference do schools make if, as some scholars have argued, they represent the broken promises of public education?[15]

What difference do schools make if—under the burden of heavy school districts and union bureaucracies, in run-down buildings, managed by self-serving politicians, stuffed by technocratic curriculum, demoralized administrators and teachers, and tested-to-death, disenfranchised students, with overworked and underpaid parents, and assailed by the world of business as another site for-profit taking—schools have abandoned the key tenets of reasonability and utopia, betraying the principles of the Enlightenment?

These are, indeed, some of the pressing questions of today and certainly, questions that the NCLB, a brainchild of neoliberalism, is unable or unwilling to answer. The answer, however, is not in a top down law of the establishment, but rather in the struggle on the streets. The answers are in the development of public spheres, in the new communities of debate and deliberation in the internet and nongovernmental organizations in civil society, and in the potential new social role of universities promoting a democratic discourse as a critic of the established power. The answer is also in the ability of teachers to remain autonomous despite teacher-proof educational models; to remain caring, critical, and well informed despite growing bureaucratic regulations of profession. The answer is finally in the social movements that will not accept the authoritarianism of reforms like the NCLB, and will continue the struggle, challenging and even practically vetoing policies of the establishment while advancing alternatives at the same time.

Considering the contradictions of social order over the centuries, the human condition was not improved by nihilists, but rather by visionaries; it was not improved by negativists, but, to paraphrase Paulo Freire, by being impatiently patient in seeking social transformation, equity, solidarity, freedom, and justice for all. Freedom was not conquered by the ruthless exercise of power, but by the imagination, passion, and utopian ideals of many anonymous women and men who chose to live and to know decent, dignifying lives despite the rule of authoritarian powers. Neoliberalism and the NCLB will not pass the test of time. We will be ready to construct a future with better social justice and a more caring and reasonable educational policy.

Part II

From Critique to Utopia

Alternatives to
Neoliberal Globalization

4 Education, Teachers' Unions and the State
The Theses of Lisbon[1]

THESIS ONE

The conflict between state and teachers' union policies hinges on the conflict between particular and universal in the constitution of the public good.

In the liberal democratic tradition, the state was always seen as representing the general interest. The state, in the tradition that arises from Hegel and Kant, remains the architect of the will of society insofar as it represents the universal public good, trying to regulate, articulate, and mediate among competing particular interests. This perception of general interests versus particular interests make the notion of the state as an independent actor, an independent referee in social struggles, as an arena for policy confrontation, the key element in the constitution of the legitimacy of the state. Even in the neo-Marxist perspective, the same notion of relative autonomy is based on the constitution of the state as the potential arbiter, independent from particular interests that will make the state the ruling committee of the bourgeoisie.

Unions, on the other hand, were seen as articulating the private, particular interests of a segment of society; that is, in the case of teachers' unions, of teachers as cultural workers. Teachers, teachers' organizations, and particularly teachers' values play a central role in the consolidation of democracy, both in school settings, through the process of socialization, and in the larger societal framework. Teachers' values, attitudes, and beliefs are central to the democratic stability and the legitimacy of democratic regimes. Thus teachers are instrumental in the transmission of a nation's collective values to children and youth. Given this role, it is not surprising that teachers become visibly upset when they perceive diminishing financial investments in public education, which is seen as a lack of state commitment to public education.

Yet, teachers' unions are different than other unions because there is a sense of building the nation and constructing the soul of the nation by working with the children of the nation. In short, teachers' unions are part and parcel of the constitution of citizenship. In that respect, they are part and parcel of the state, particularly when they establish, as normalism did for so long, an alliance with basic tenets of the constitution of civil society and, more specifically, the nation, *la patria*, etc.

Even if one considers unions as not really a part of a theory of the state but rather a representative of a sizable segment of civil society, one ought to recognize that unions, by and large, respond to a constituency of workers, and act with a mandate delegated by the workers, and thus specific interests. Yet, when teachers' unions march on Congress as CTERA[2] did, or argue back and forth with the government against the process of privatization, or create conditions for challenging curriculum policies that are not seen as advancing the cause of public education, or challenge the underfunding of education, unions act not as representatives of the private interest or the particular, but on behalf of the public interest as the universal good.

This practice, however, has to do with the previous socialization of teachers' unions in the defense of public education, a socialization that, with the difficulties faced in the past while negotiating with state institutions, is part of the legacy of liberalism (the state as constructing the nation, and the teacher as a missionary).

THESIS TWO

The particular/universal dualism becomes even more pronounced in the context of globalization, therefore giving the unions a more powerful role in challenging free trade deals and the role of the state in opening the economy, and inserting the economy and culture as well as politics in the process of globalization.

Disregarding how one understands the process of globalization, teachers and the educational system are subject to the dynamics of globalization in different ways. There are, as argued in Burbules and Torres, economic and cultural characteristics of globalization.[3] One of the key components of the discussion on globalization nowadays is the role that the neoliberal state plays in the constitution of the social imagination of contemporary capitalist societies, particularly the role it plays in the operation of the system of public education.

As it has been argued in Burbules and Torres, a neoliberal version of globalization is reflected in the educational agenda that privileges "if not directly imposes, particular policies for evaluation, financing, assessment, standards, teachers' training, curriculum, instruction and testing."[4] This international agenda of education, supported by governments, international and bilateral international organizations, is somewhat (more firmly in some cases than in others) challenged by teachers' unions.

Burbules and Torres have argued that:

In the face of such pressures, more study is needed about local responses to defend public education against the introduction of pure market mechanisms to regulate educational exchanges and other policies that seek to reduce state sponsorship and financing and to impose management and efficiency models borrowed from the business sector as a framework for educational decisionmaking.[5]

Therefore, the nation and the state now appear to be representing the world of the universal (or acting on behalf of the universal rather than the particular set of interests) and the market, which could indeed be thought of as another kind of particular universal, reflecting a collection of specific interests. Unions, fighting to preserve public education from becoming a market education, are challenging the type of insertion of the economy, politics, and culture in the process of globalization, challenging the role of the state, and challenging the international agenda for investment, research, and evaluation in educational policy.

An interesting contradiction is the following: while the state argues that it still represents the universal and therefore, as the "technology of domination" it controls education,[6] the reliance on the market by state institutions opens up avenues to challenge the same role that the state has played in the past, creating all sort of noises in the system, and opening the state's role to challenges by other entities in the civil society. Therefore, institutions such as unions, which are supposed to pursue and defend private interests, are replacing the universal role of the state in the defense of public education. Yet, it is the role allocated by the state to the unions in the past that makes the union's present practice so solid compared to the current state practices that contradict the past history of state involvement in education.

THESIS THREE

The new role of teachers' unions is neither corporatist nor populist, nor just a defense of welfare state policies. The new role of teachers' unions is the creation of a public sphere for policy deliberation (the White Tent Effect of CTERA).[7]

This new role of teachers' unions, with a greater involvement in policy making and curriculum, reveals that by definition cannot be corporatist or populist (which is also a function of the political regime), but it is at the same time not necessarily part of welfare state policies. Why? Though not totally clear, it is not corporatist or populist because it challenges the same way the state is organizing neoliberal policies in education, social welfare, and the economy. It is not populist because it doesn't rely in the presence of charismatic leadership, negotiations at the parliamentary level on new mechanisms of representation and social distribution. Neither attempts to develop a mass social movement for specific political purposes. While unions are, by nature, not proactive but reactive, in their defense of public education, they draw the line more often on moral and ethical imperatives than in terms of political calculation. The process of privatization and the international agenda of neoliberalism are difficult pills to swallow if they are going to fulfill their self-assigned functions.

Yet, while creatures of the welfare state in many ways, some of the recent developments in some countries, which have teachers' unions acting in concert with other institutional referents of civil society, show that teacher unions are pursuing the creation of public spheres rather than the creation of welfare state niches for their own demands.

THESIS FOUR

The role of unions in challenging state policies has implications at the level of "producing," distributing, and consuming social capital in democratic civil societies.

Social capital can be simply described as the product of a set of enforceable norms shared among members of a community, with a great deal of trust among themselves, and who have developed an elaborate network of interactions that contributes to social action. It is relevant to point out that one of the most important elements of 'professional unionism' or 'new realism' is a shift from confrontational labor relations to a more collaborative approach.[8]

It is clear that relying solely on the market for public policy is problematic. Choice and deregulated educational markets are thought of as increasing exchange efficiency and productive efficiency.[9] Indeed:

> These economic exchanges, however, represent a 'search for universally applicable hypotheses . . . which transcend institutional, systematic and historical variations and . . . are abstracted from social organizations and cultural patterns.[10]

This is crucial because the abstract logic of the market appears as a universal logic to be placed upon all policy exchanges, but it ignores the institutional logics, which are embedded in the historical process of a given society. Institutionalization and history play major roles in filtering structural dynamics and logics. Therefore, the universal, as part of the market behavior, becomes simple a collection of particular goals, as outlined in the previous thesis. The question is how could this affect the discussion on social capital? Here then, Peter, Marshall, and Fitzimons have an interesting point confronting the formation of education policy with the roles of education in capitalist societies:

A market is simply not an allocative device: it is also a system for creating and measuring value, for producing and ordering preferences that in turn become embedded in culture. It is, therefore, a political device. By virtue of these ambient processes of cultural production, the market (in a circular logic) generates the very standards, including exchange efficiency, that neoclassical economists employ to evaluate market outcomes. Education, for example, is as much an investment in human capital formation, cultural property, social capital, and competitive advantage as it is consumption choice about which school a child will attend.[11]

One of the key concerns in contemporary social theory is to analyze how the notion of social capital can be instrumental in promoting new domains of political negotiation, new models of solidarity and conflict resolution, and new perspectives on the constitution of a richer, more textured network of social action, which could address some of the key problems of contemporary democracies. Obviously these problems cannot be addressed by a single research agenda, and there is a risk that social capital could be seen as a one-size-fits-all solution to the many dilemmas of contemporary democratic societies. However, social capital is, first and foremost, a heuristic device that can be used to explore the role of primary and secondary organizations in the articulation of social interactions in society. We have taken advantage of this heuristic sociological concept in our research in order to help understand what role, if any, education (particularly educational policies and teachers' unions) could play in the establishment of rational patterns of social interaction (what Habermas would like to term *communicative rationality*) and new symbolic scenarios and practices for achieving shared notions of the 'good society.'

The field of education offers a privileged vantage point from which to examine the production, distribution, consumption, and even deterioration of social capital in capitalist democratic societies. Thus, a central part of our analysis has dealt with the issue of the constitution, reconstitution, and eventual destruction of social capital in the production of educational policy and the interaction between states and teachers' organizations. The focus of this inquiry has been comparative and policy-oriented, dealing with the impact of school reform agendas on the lives of teachers and teachers' unions.

THESIS FIVE

The new role of teachers' unions in promoting a public sphere in the defense of public education has given teachers and teachers' unions a new credibility in terms of their political capital. They have increased their political capital but not at the expense of diminishing their ability to contribute social capital in capitalist democracies.

One may simply argue that the accumulation of political capital is a function of how politics are played in a given society, what are the key actors in influencing decisions, and how exchanges in the process of governing are being processed by central units in the constitution of decision making. In short, political capital is not only an outcome of processes of coalition building (e.g., negotiation) or confrontation, but it is the result of influence, prestige, legitimacy, and resource mobilization. In all these areas, over the last decade, teachers' unions have accumulated more prestige, legitimacy, influence, and resource mobilization in some societies compared with their past experience (Argentina and Korea are exemplary in this respect; Canada perhaps is a more borderline case; and Mexico, Japan, and the United States come down on the lukewarm side of the thesis).

Key questions are the following: Why and how could teachers' unions accumulate political capital at the expense of the political capital of the state? There are sets of arguments that can be validated.

First, teaching is not the most profitable profession in capitalist societies, yet it is a profession in which there is a delicate balance between production and distribution, discipline and learning, and caring and moral education and education for production. Since education involves working with children (someone else's children and youth), teachers are empowered by society to look after these children when parents are not there (acting *in locus parenti*). This is a role that was originally taken over by the state in the nineteenth century, but it is indeed performed by teachers, who are the concrete actors in the process of learning. Teachers, who are not the best paid professionals in society (here the contradiction between professionalism and unionism is flagrant), in some cases, are professionals who use the teaching profession as a 'one stop' institution, or a 'lay over' institution, to use the terminology of frequent flyers, in their development of professional careers. In short, a most meaningful profession, but not one of the best paid. This factor gives credibility to the idea of a teacher vocation, and some sort of involvement and contributions beyond the enacted rewards of the profession.

Second, not only are teachers not the most rentable professionals, but they are also locally (state) certified. This, in turn, creates all sorts of constraints, as well as opportunities, given the dynamics of local certification, evaluation of performance, and the overall process of learning evaluation.

Third, teachers as professionals and teachers' unions are protected from international competition. One the one hand, local certification makes this protection stronger. On the other hand, the work on children, nation, and values make the ability to import foreign workers to ease labor shortages (as with the case of bilingual teachers in the United States) quite unlikely and a source of conflict even if it were possible. Outside the circuits of globalization, teachers and teachers' unions become one of the most evident 'national' markets and 'national' professions.

Fourth, though outside the circuit of globalization in terms of job and market competition, teachers, and education in general, are supposed to prepare people for competing in international markets. This poses an intriguing dilemma: How can people who feel happily excluded from the risks of labor globalization in their own labor niches prepare other people to take advantage of labor opportunities in increasingly globalized markets?

Fifth, teachers are key in promoting the training of human resources to a growingly globalized world while, at the same time they have been agents of some sort of globalization, internationalization, or enlightenment, perhaps the best descriptor. Their action in their classrooms, in the perspective of the liberal enlightenment is not to promote discrete, idiosyncratic behavior, but to promote cultural tolerance, cultural understanding, and a greater notion of knowledge creation as an international and universal scientific process. Teachers are by definition great internationalizers in society, great globalizers in culture. Teachers as cultural workers are situated at the center of the dilemmas of globalization and national autonomy.

Sixth, and finally, teachers are key to the constitution of principles of order in growingly chaotic societies as long as they work with ideological materials, norms, perspectives, analyses, mores, civics, discipline, etc. These principles of order may lead, particularly in the role of teachers' unions, to growing polarization and conflict or, conversely, they may lead to growing consensus and collaboration. This, of course, intersects with the role of teachers and teachers' organizations as institutions that produce, distribute, and consume social capital (thesis four).

In closing, a not-so-careful reading of the newspapers in the world will clearly show that the political capital of the state is diminishing quite rapidly, a case in point is the great debate in Mexico, with people taking to the streets with their dissatisfaction of Mexican civil society and the decision from the Mexican state to move into line with the international changes on daytime savings in energy—changing the hour. There are many examples of this nature about the distrust of state policies. In the past, the state was able to pursue an agenda of reform simply by pushing its legitimacy either as part of comprehensive rational planning based on political participation (the notion of expertise applying science to planning), or legalization through the court systems.

Clearly these policies of compensatory legitimizing are failing now, the governability of democratic societies becoming even more convoluted and difficult, and in this context, emergent units of civil society, such as unions, may be able to accumulate political capital at the expense of the political capital of the state. Yet, there are several conditions necessary for this to occur: that these units achieve the level of legitimacy that the state has been losing progressively; that they speak for the general interest of the overall population, and not for specific interests of a given group; and finally, that they are able to contribute to the social capital of capitalist societies in measurable, demonstrable, and effective ways. Educational unions are in an enviable position to achieve these goals with relatively few costs for their position in the political system, their leadership, and their membership.

5 The Political Pedagogy of Paulo Freire[1]

In Memoriam Paulo Reglus Neves Freire (1921–1997)

THIS BOOK AND ITS AUTHOR

For the progressive educators, tomorrow is not unyielding.

—Freire, Politics and Education

I first discussed the translation and publication of this book, originally published in Portuguese in 1996, with Paulo Freire two years ago at his house in São Paulo. We just had finished one more session of conversations and interviews that I had with him—with surprising regularity, given his schedule and mine—for the last two decades . These conversations between friends were also part of a book about his life and work that I have been postponing for too long. It was a wonderful evening in the company of Paulo and Moacir Gadotti, and we shared the wonderful Brazilian *aguardiente* that Paulo liked so much, *casasha*, while we chatted in a typical, animated Latin American fashion, surrounded by Paulo's art, books, and *honoris causa* diplomas.

He graciously signed a contract authorizing the Latin American Center at UCLA to publish his work. He had been to UCLA several times in the past decade. In fact, it was outside the Graduate School of Education and Information Studies at UCLA, on the Kerkoff patio after a lecture on the 12 of April 1991, that Paulo Freire suggested to Moacir Gadotti and I , to create the Paulo Freire Institute to continue his educational theories and concrete educational interventions. The afternoon of April 12, the Paulo Freire Institute was born, with its principal branch in São Paulo. Today, it numbers more than 21 scholarly nuclei in 18 countries.[2]

Freire very much liked the idea that the Latin American Center would publish some of his work for the English-speaking reader. Indeed, this book was one of the key subjects of conversation in our last telephone exchange, two weeks before his unexpected death.

Paulo Reglus Neves Freire was born in Recife, Brazil, on September 19, 1921, and died of heart failure in São Paulo, Brazil, on May 2, 1997. Paulo was our friend, a wonderful and spiritual man who inspired a whole generation of critical educators. He was a pedagogue who expanded our perceptions of the world, nourished our will, enlightened our awareness of the causes and consequences of human suffering, and illuminated the need to develop an ethical and utopian pedagogy for social change. His death has left us with memories of his gestures and passionate voice, his white bearded face resembling a prophet, and his marvelous Socratic books.

Paulo taught us that domination, aggression, and violence are an intrinsic part of human and social life. Paulo argued that few human encounters are exempt from oppression of one kind or another because by virtue of race, class, or gender, people tend to be victims and/or perpetrators of oppression. He stressed that racism, sexism, or class exploitation are the most salient forms of dominance and oppression, but he also recognized that oppression exists on the grounds of religious beliefs, political affiliation, national origin, age, size, and physical and intellectual handicaps.

Paulo, beginning with a psychology of oppression influenced by the works of psychotherapists such as Freud, Jung, Adler, Fanon, and Fromm, developed a "Pedagogy of the Oppressed." He believed that education could improve the human condition, counteracting the effects of a psychology of oppression and ultimately contributing to what he considered the "ontological vocation of mankind": humanization. In the introduction to his widely acclaimed *Pedagogy of the Oppressed,* he argued that:

> From these pages I hope at least the following will endure: my trust in the people, and my faith in men and women and in the creation of a world in which it will be easier to love.[3]

Paulo was known as a philosopher and theoretician of education, never separating theory from praxis. He attempted to implement his educational philosophy on many occasions, including his famous experience as an adviser to the revolutionary government of Guinea-Bissau in the mid-seventies, which resulted in one of his most popular books, *Pedagogy in Process: The Letters to Guinea-Bissau.* His appointment as Secretary of Education of the City of São Paulo in January 1989 created a unique opportunity for him to implement his ideas in his own country. When the Partido Dos Trabalhadores (Worker's Party, or PT) won the municipal elections in São Paulo in 1988, a natural choice for the Secretary of Education was Paulo Freire, a well-known Brazilian socialist pedagogue, and one of the originators of popular education in Latin America who also inspired the constitution of Theology of Liberation. A member of the party since 1979, and President of the Fundação Wilson Pinhero—a kind of Workers' University sponsored by the Workers' Party in São Paulo—Secretary of Education Paulo Freire took charge of 654 schools with 700,000 students, from K1-8, and also engaged in adult education and literacy training in the City of São Paulo, one of the megalopolises of Latin America. The reverberations of his policy work are still felt in São Paulo due to the implementation of many of his administration's innovations in curriculum, teacher training, school governance, and literacy training, which linked social movements with the state.

Throughout his life, Paulo became one of the most recognized pedagogues associated with progressive causes, the educational New Left, and Critical Pedagogy. Given the wide range of his philosophical and educational contributions, the impact of Freire's work cannot be restricted to literacy training or adult education. Problem-posing education, or the methodology for thematic research—two of the main theoretical and methodological innovations resulting from Freire's work—have been implemented not only in social studies and curriculum studies in adult education, secondary education, and higher education, but also in such diverse subjects as the teaching of mathematics and physics, educational planning, feminist studies, romance languages, educational psychology, and so forth.

In this book that the readers have in their hands, Paulo offers us his meta-language, his poetics, and his epistemology of curiosity. Like Antonio Gramsci in his *Quaderni del Carcere,* Paulo offers a series of extremely insightful yet fragmented reflections that need to be studied very seriously. He talks challengingly about progressive or radical post-modernism and about the need to uphold the truth; and yet, Paulo argues not against grand narratives but against totalizing certainties. He speaks passionately for school autonomy and against neoliberalism. He argues for an education of truth, utopia, creative imagination, and tolerance. This is another of his books, perhaps one of the last ones to be translated into English, that will help us think and act politically and pedagogically in a dialectic of unity in diversity intimately linked to the authenticity of Paulo's life, thought, and work.

I found myself on many occasions staring at a page of the manuscript and wondering what are the political and intellectual as well as pedagogical implications of phrases like this one, beautifully crafted through Paulo's poetic language and yet heavily influenced by the work of Eric Fromm: "Authoritarianism is like necrophilia, just as a coherently democratic progressive is like biofilia."[4] Or for instance, what are the political and epistemological implications of another phrase reflecting his obsession for the question of the directedness of education:

> The directedness of educational practice, that allows it to position itself and pursue certain outcomes—a dream, a utopia—does not permit its neutrality. The impossibility of being neutral has nothing to do with the arbitrary imposition that the authoritarian educator makes on "his" or "her" learners.[5]

Or let us consider what the implications of Paulo's statement on the question of translation are, which can boomerang, in fact, and thus reverberate throughout the whole edifice of intellectual practice:

> To read a book, for example, in Portuguese translation, because you don't know the native language of the author well enough but still cite from that translated version is neither an ethical nor a respectable action.[6]

I began the introductory study on the political pedagogy of Paulo Freire that follows shortly before Paulo's death. He was waiting to see this study before the book went to press, but this was not meant to be.[7] What the reader will find in this book is another attempt by Paulo to render more clarity to his understanding of the connections between politics and education, which are, no doubt, at the heart of the educational dilemmas of our time.

THE JOURNEY

> I fulfill my mission as an educator when, "fighting" to convince learners of the revelation of truth, I myself become transparent, allowing my students the possibility of arguing with the ideas of my discourse. I fulfill my mission as an educator when I reveal, finally, my tolerance in the face of those who are different from me.[8]

Intellectual work, and particularly writing about culture and education, is a journey of discovery. Authors endlessly struggle to find the right phrase, the right metaphor or analogy, the right concept to underscore the analysis, the appropriate narrative and rhetorical strategy to bring to life theory, research, and praxis.

This journey is a process of learning, and a difficult one. Initial intuitions and convictions are modified, broadened, and strengthened. Arguments take on solidity; new horizons soon open up when deficiencies and naive initial perceptions are corrected or new evidence is gathered and assessed. Yet, at the same time that an author begins to delve into contradictory themes, reality is pressing the flesh, so to speak; making those themes more than just an intellectual preoccupation but a life quest for knowledge. Despite facing similar hurdles, however, not every writer confronts the same challenges nor can they offer similar venues of expression or similar genres.

This is not necessarily because of different personal narratives or stylistic differences—although they play a role—but because ideology, values, and *weltanschuung* matter. If an author considers the education of the oppressed and dominated sectors from a critical perspective, sharing the sense of outrage and the sensibility and compassion for the poor and their living conditions may prompt this intellectual journey to become even more radical over time. That is, not just to become a description or analysis, but a social intervention in the process of social transformation.

Freire said it very well in this book:

> I can affirm that the lived practices that evolved over these ten years reinforced intuitions that I had since my youth and which become increasingly confirmed during my professional experience. One of these: one really works in favor of the popular classes if one works *with them*, discussing their dreams, desires, frustrations, fears and joys.[9]

This is, in brief, the intellectual path of Paulo Freire's political pedagogy, in the context of the pedagogical and political problems that informed his work.[10]

EDUCATION AND CONSCIOUSNESS

> Teachers do not teach only subject matter. Through their practice, they also teach how to think critically. If we are progressive, then to teach, for us, is not to deposit packages in the vacant consciousness of learners.[11]

Early on in his research, Freire studied the organization of the class consciousness of the oppressed, focusing on concrete social processes while, at the same time, searching for an effective transformation of the structures of oppression. In so doing, his focus was always educational and cultural. While Paulo Freire's thought requires a number of historical (theoretical and strategic) mediations for its implementation in pedagogical, organizational, and political terms, it is, from its very beginning, an eminently political thought. For Freire, politics, power, and education are an indissoluble unit. As a set of relationships, they interpenetrate each other.[12]

Paulo Freire says this very nicely in this book:

> The comprehension of the limits of educational practice absolutely requires political clarity on the part of educators in relation to their project. It demands that the educator assumes the political nature of his/her practice. It is not enough to say that education is a political act just as it is not enough to say that political acts are also educative. It is necessary to truly assume the political nature of education. I cannot consider myself progressive if I understand school space to be something neutral, with limited or no relation to class struggle, in which students are seen only as learners of limited domains of knowledge which I will imbue with magic power. I cannot recognize the limits of the political-educative practice in which I am involved if I don't know, if I am not clear about in whose favor I work. Clarifying the question of in whose favor I practice, puts me in a certain position, which is related

to class, in which I devise against whom I practice and, necessarily, for what reasons I practice—that is, the dream, the type of society on whose behalf I would like to intervene, act, and participate.[13]

The political implications of Freirean thought have been recognized by several authors.[14] In terms of the foundations of his method, Freire has even been associated in his beginnings with Socratic mayéutica,[15] and undoubtedly, his constant incursions in writing dialogical books proved to be one of his pedagogical and political obsessions.[16] As it is the case in the Freirean proposals, for Socrates, the conquest of knowledge is brought about through the free exercise of consciousness. Nevertheless, the particularity that distinguishes the Freirean method and philosophy from Socratic mayéutica, despite their common foundations, is rooted in the fact that the participants of the dialogue in the circle of culture are common men and women, not a minority of aristocrats dedicated to *otium* and speculation, as opposed to the *negotium*.[17] Not surprisingly, in this book Freire invites us to avoid the temptation to overvalue science and devalue common sense.

For the participants in a Freirean-inspired educational dialogue, the words that are said (and learned) have a vital imprint. Participants in the cultural circles of popular education speak of their work or their lack of work and the pains of unemployment. They speak about their pains and joys, their sickness and alienation, their struggles and hopes, and their dreams. For this reason, the affirmation made by Brazilian political scientist, Francisco C. Weffort, in his introductory remarks to the first edition of *Educación como práctica de la libertad* in 1969 even today continues to hold validity.[18] He argues that:

> Thus these mayéutica for the masses compromise from the start the educators and the person he or she educates, as concrete men and women, who can never be limited to the strict learning of techniques and abstract notions. The starting point for work in the cultural circles is in assuming freedom and criticism as woman's and man's way of being.[19]

EDUCATION AND CONSCIENTIZATION

The question of language, fundamentally, is a question of class.[20]

The education that Freire proposed to his readers in his first book, *Education as the Practice of Freedom,* and what has reverberated throughout his life work, could be defined succinctly as an education for liberation and for political and social responsibility. These claims are reaffirmed throughout this book.

Without a doubt, this proposal is in communion with all the great modern educators such as Makarenko, Celestin Freinet, Karl Rogers, John Dewey, and many others. The basic objectives from which the Freirian educational praxis evolved sought first to realize an age-old Brazilian aspiration—the overcoming of illiteracy among the country's popular sectors[21]—and second, strove to achieve the extension and enhancement of democracy through popular educational participation. It is around these two objectives that the dynamism Paulo Freire imprints on his task of increasing literacy has meaning.

Three decades later, his experiences in Brazil as Secretary of Education from 1989–1991 will confirm that this political pedagogy can, and indeed did, make possible one of the most fascinating experiences of policy making, curriculum development, and school governance in the region, and perhaps internationally.[22]

As Weffort rightly indicated almost four decades ago:

> A pedagogy structured in a cultural circle as the site of a free and critical practice cannot be viewed as yet one more idealization of freedom. The dimensions of meaning and human practice are found in the binding unity of its foundations. It is thus that an educational vision cannot keep from being, at the same time, a criticism of the real oppression in which men and women live and an expression of their struggle to free themselves . . . Theory and denouncement nourish one another mutually in the same way that cultural circles and learning in discussion on the notion of work and culture are never separate from the growth of awareness, since they are realized in the very process of this growth of awareness. This conscientization often signifies the start of the search for a fighting stance. The understanding of this pedagogy in its practical, political, and social dimension, requires, therefore, clarity with respect to this fundamental aspect; the idea of freedom only takes on full meaning when it is in communion with men's and women's concrete struggle to free themselves.[23]

This long paragraph by Weffort brings us closer to Freire's thoughts about the intimate unity between education and conscientization, which unveils, in Freire's analysis, the intimate connection between politics and education. Freire developed this notion of education for conscientization in many of his works throughout his life.[24] His view, indeed, is intimately connected to his philosophy, which is found at the intersection of some of the most vibrant philosophical currents of the twentieth century, including Marxism, Phenomenology, Existentialism, Christian Personalism, and Hegelianism.[25]

RADICAL DEMOCRACY

Gender cannot explain everything. Neither can race, nor can class. A labor leader, audacious and entrepreneurial, wizened in the struggle for liberty, who treats his partner as a sexual object is as incoherent as a feminist white leader who disparages a Black agrarian worker, or a progressive intellectual that speaks to workers rather than pushing himself to speak *with* them.[26]

It would be too simplistic to attribute Freire's notion of a political pedagogy to his analytical perspective linked to the New Left. That is, his political pedagogy does not rest simply on an ideological preference, but rather on a strong and unqualified democratic impulse. Like it or not, Freire reminds us that education is a political activity, and that any serious political activity is educational. However, at the same time, he invites us to transcend this assertion, and to consider the full range of implications of the relationships between education and politics. For instance, and not surprisingly, political philosophy helps us to identify the connections between theories of the state, theories of citizenship, theories of democracy, and theories of education, connections that are intimately linked to the Freirean research, political, and practical agendas.[27]

Yet, this connection between politics and education has been recognized by many authors who do not share the kind of philosophical perceptions that Freire espoused. For instance, from the liberal trenches, Amy Gutmann has persuasively argued that education for citizenship should focus on the justification of rights rather than responsibilities, but at the same time, schools should foster general virtues (courage, lawfulness, loyalty), social virtues (independence, open mindedness), economic virtues (work ethic, capacity to delay self-gratification), and political virtues (capacity to discern, capacity to criticize). From this perspective, schools should teach children how to engage in the kind of critical reasoning and moral perspective that defines public reasonableness.[28]

Freire teaches us that the connections between education and politics cannot be theorized only in terms of the intersections between power and education, or exclusively in terms of the relationships between power and knowledge; a theorizing that, to be sure, has permeated Freire's contributions. While Freire has tirelessly highlighted the "politicity of education," he has simultaneously urged us in this book, and in countless other works, to understand the relationships between education and citizenship training, and particularly to illuminate the historical, normative, and ontological foundations of democratic education and citizenship rights and responsibilities.

Democratic education should also consider civic virtues, as outlined previously in Gutmann's position. These civic virtues will not only constitute the citizen, but will enhance the chances of democracy to function in contemporary capitalist societies because "citizenship must play an independent normative role in any plausible political theory and that the promotion of responsible citizenship is an urgent aim of public policy."[29] Yes, education for citizenship will be central to the aim of the Freirean project. Alas, citizenship education is built as part of radical democratic project and as part and parcel of a utopian democratic education.

UTOPIAN DEMOCRATIC EDUCATION

> When I was Municipal Secretary of Education for São Paulo I was obviously committed to developing and administration that, in coherence with our political dream and our utopia, would seriously consider the question of popular participation in school . . . It was necessary to democratize power, to recognize the right of the voice of students and teachers, to diminish the personal power of the directors, and to create new instances of power with the School Councils. . . . [30]

For Freire, debates about education and democracy should deal, ultimately, with the notion of utopia. Indeed, his proposal of an education for liberation still resonates because of its boldness and utopian nature. He says, with Hegelian overtones, that:

> Truly, only the oppressed are able to conceive of a future totally distinct from their present, insofar as they arrive at a consciousness of a dominated class. The oppressors, as the dominating class, cannot conceive of the future unless it is the preservation of their present as oppressors. In this way, whereas the future of the oppressed consists in the revolutionary transformation of society, without which their liberation will not be verified, the oppressor's future consists in the simple modernization of society, which permits the continuation of its class supremacy. [31]

While this statement has the flavor of the utopian discussions of the sixties in Latin America, asking for ways to create more just and inform and educate societies in the midst of a region besieged by political activism, violence, and the arrogance of the elites in power, Freire's voice resonates with authenticity and love, a perspective that is still firmly rooted in his last works, including his books *Pedagogy of Hope* and *Letters to Cristina* (one of his latest contributions to the democratic conversation about education), and in this book, which we are bringing to the English-speaking reader shortly after Freire's death. This conversation, as far as Freire was concerned, always related to teachers and their social, political, and pedagogical imagination. He wanted teachers who will accept the utopia of a new education, a new society, and a new human being who pursues an egalitarian path of solidarity.

This utopian factor implies a double tension: announcement and denouncement. Insofar as the teacher carries out his or her utopian role, he or she is turned into a dangerous prophet for the system. Rather than performing the role of the functionary who reproduces the elements of the ideological consciousness of the mode of production, the educator becomes a cultural critic and education becomes a public sphere, a theater for public deliberation controlled neither by the state nor the market. According to Freire, when educators collaborate in the organization of the oppressed sectors, educators and popular classes can come to be liberated. Consequently, Freirean political pedagogy, the pedagogy of the oppressed, is undoubtedly a working-class pedagogy, as Freire emphasizes throughout this book. The question that immediately arises is the following: what are the effects of a pedagogy of class? Weffort, in reference to the early beginnings of the Freire's political philosophy of education and method, says:

> But, if a pedagogy of freedom outlines the germ of revolt, not for this reason would it be correct to affirm that revolt is found among the aims of the educator. If it happens, it is hardly and exclusively because conscientization discerns a real situation in which the most frequent givens are struggle and violence. To conscientize in no way means to ideologize or propose words of order. If conscientization opens the way to the expression of social insatisfactions it is because there are real components of a situation of oppression: many are the workers who, having just acquired literacy, join labor movements or unions, and this is because, to them, it seems to be the legitimate path for the defense of their interest and those of their workmates: finally, if conscientization of the popular classes signifies political radicalization, this is simply because the popular classes are radical. . . . [32]

Here we arrive at an important point, especially in terms of political theory: the process of conscientization operates predominantly as part and parcel of the subjective factors for social change. Conscientization clears the way for a critical understanding of the situation of oppression and the overcoming of it. This critical consciousness emerges within a specific context of systemic contradictions and class struggle, thus allowing not only the surfacing of the radicalism of the popular classes, but also the social contradictions and the repression of the popular sectors by social structures and elites that impede social and political participation. This critical consciousness then carries, with unequivocal signs, the intent for the radical transformation of the political system, and may even postulate the transformation of the capitalist mode of production itself.

Just as in Paulo Freire's early writings, in which education was an instrumental factor to "help man and woman to reflect upon his or her ontological vocation of subject," i.e., to help build a critical consciousness of his or her reality (as much of its determinations as of its potentialities), the political implication, though directly conditioned by the double subjective–objective dialectics mentioned above, moved over to another plane. Let us explain ourselves. Freire, though totally aware of the political implications of a liberating education, was also aware of the contradictions of this education. On the one hand, there is always the possibility of the manipulation and ideologizing of consciousness (i.e., to promote education and methodologies at the service of a project of domination). On the other hand, Freire believed that a certain connection could be established between educational praxis and political praxis *stricto sensu*. It was incumbent on the educator, fundamentally, to develop a project of literacy training and conscientization, while the "professional" politician was in charge of realizing the task of organizing the oppressed sectors in terms of political structures.[33]

Nevertheless, when Freire's thought became more radical, he began to break this dichotomy, especially when he said that:

> Upon reducing expressions such as "humanism," "humanization," "human promotion" to abstract categories, they are emptied of their real meaning. They become a blah-blah-blah whose only merit is to serve the reactionary forces. In effect, a "humanization" without liberation is absolutely not possible, just as there is no freedom without a revolutionary transformation of the class society, where this humanization cannot be brought about.[34]

POLITICAL EDUCATION, POLITICAL REVOLUTION

> . . . Trying to create a popular education was obviously much easier for us in the administration than for those progressive educators that assume democratic projects under an authoritarian administration that always react to democracy as a risk and to creativity as if it were the devil in the presence of the cross.[35]

In many writings and interventions, Freire postulated that there is no educational revolution without political revolution. No educational action can provoke a revolution of power. Education is not merely instrumental; rather, it is a field of ideological struggles that must be waged. It is nearly impossible to bring about a liberating cultural action with the oppressed sectors before the taking of power; however, it is possible to carry out educational tasks and programs, which constitute the true seeds of the organization of the popular sectors. When the moment arrives in which a radical political switch can take place, then the space for democratic reforms may be opened. In his earlier work, he takes the cultural revolution in China as a model in several ways because such a revolution would make these educational tasks compatible with an action of formal and systematic education. This "compatibilization" would indeed give over to a true and liberating cultural action.[36]

This political process of conscientization has been perceived by many authors. For example, Fausto Franco says:

Finally, a fourth step already initiated somehow from the beginnings of his pedagogical trek is characterized by two well defined traits: the making explicit of certain socio-analytic assumptions in which to base himself and, more concretely, the admission of social classes as the area in which the oppression of men is carried out; the identification of political consciousness with class consciousness and the open incorporation of certain elements of Marxism in his analysis of reality.[37]

Freire asserts, confirming this perspective, that:

When an illiterate from Angicos, speaking in front of President Goulart . . . declared that he was no longer "Masa" but "gente," that was not only a sentence: he consciously affirmed an option. He choose a decisive participation that only the people have and he rejected the emotional dimension of the masses. He was politicized.[38]

The political vocabulary of ideas that animates the conscientizing process, though repeated, does not cease to be important in Freire's work. Our author summarized it in one sentence, resembling Ernesto "Che" Guevara political journey:

To be a revolutionary means to oppose oneself to oppression and exploitation and to be in favor of the liberation of the oppressed classes, in concrete terms and not in idealistic terms.[39]

Thus the process of politicization in the revolution of consciousness may imply for Freire an option for the building up of a vanguard, of a revolutionary leadership, when he states:

The organization of the popular masses into classes is the process through which the revolutionary leadership, like the masses, has been deprived of speaking its mind and establishes the learning of the pronunciation of the world.[40]

Years ago I said that in the confusion of today's world, educators can be with Freire or against Freire, but not without Freire. This book is another proof. His life taught us the meaning of honesty, decency, creativity, and struggle. His death taught us so many things that cannot be captured in a sentence, and even if Paulo is no longer with us, we remember him and are grateful for his life, his work, and the inspiration they give us.

6 Critical Social Theory and Educational Research

INTRODUCTION

This chapter assumes that the legacy of Critical Social Theory has made impressive contributions to our understanding of the social sciences, particularly linking critique and utopia. Yet it is evident that these contributions have not yet reached full force in the domain of education, particularly educational establishments and policy formation.

This situation may be the product of historical and political reasons. After all, theories are shaped, enunciated, practiced, formulated, and refuted in the context of learning and political communities. One may argue, following Kantian formulations, that the deployment of reason has a history, admitting that the degree to which individuals may participate in its optimal use has been historically contingent. (Morrow & Torres, 2002: 20).

It is surely would not be an overstatement to argue that, in the United States, a great number of professionals in the field of education share neoliberal or neoconservative positions as their professional 'common sense.' Additionally, the educational establishment endorses principles of science, which have been articulated by some formulation of positivism as the predominant scientific paradigm in educational planning.[1] There are many other analytical and political options to neoliberalism and positivism, including constructivism[2] and Critical Social Theory.

However, as it becomes clear in the concluding section, it is up to intellectuals to embrace specific projects of social reform. For critical intellectuals, Critical Social Theory may offer privileged vantage points and exciting perspectives.

Looking at the world of politics, in which, despite democratic traditions, a 'winner takes it all' mentality and the idea of winning at any price are the guiding ethics, one may become demoralized. How we can practice a model of critical education—which is in itself a model of political education and a moral model in normative terms—when politics in capitalist democracies, and its reverberation in mass media, postulate vastly antagonistic political values, principles, and practices?

There are many reasons for dismay. A fundamental one is the emerging role of the United States as a neo-imperialist country[3], acting as the sole superpower, and imposing—using the strength of its military—a new *Pax*

Americana on the world. It is a model of international dominance based on the premises of "humanist militarism,"[4] isolation of its international politics, rejecting international treaties such as the Kyoto Protocol, the withdrawal from the Anti-Ballistic Missile Treaty, the scuttling of the Land Mine Treaty and the Comprehensive Test Ban Treaty,[5] and aggressiveness toward perceived enemies of a democracy and a freedom hardly fully practiced in the country and abroad.

Critical Social Theory offers some tools for discussion and political strategy. However, things need to be placed in perspective. Given the neo-imperialist position of the United States in the world system, a Critical Social Theory analysis will argue that it is insufficient to claim that quality and equality of education should be achieved in US society by eliminating the discrimination and inequality based on class, gender, race, or sexual orientation, to name just a few. Even if these processes of discrimination in education, by some miraculous factor, disappear tomorrow or be drastically ameliorated, the most significant questions about the lack of democratic behavior by the US as a superpower will continue to plague the work of conscious scholars who believe that social justice cannot be achieved without peace.

Hence, what difference does our work make? We struggle to achieve classroom environments and democratic dialogue where racism, sexism, classism, and sexual or religious discrimination do not exist, classrooms where inequality doesn't take place. We also strive for educational environments where domination and exploitation could be challenged by the logic of communicative rationality á la Habermas, hoping that this practice will reach beyond the classroom into civil society and the state. However, many of our students (poor, minority, and now in growing numbers, women) who barely finish high school end up joining the Armed Forces, endorsing an ethic of destruction of the enemy, honoring death as a way of life, and accepting the glamour of war as their professional outlook.

Make no mistake: Critical educators ask those questions out of patriotism and honesty despite the growing conservative reaction depicted in the present administration that is creating an epistemology of fear in academia through policing and controls hitherto not seen since Macartism.[6] In times like this more than ever, educators should ask themselves, following Paulo Freire, for whom they work and against whom they work. A basic premise of this task is to challenge the dominant paradigm of instrumental rationality in education.

THE DOMINANT PARADIGM OF INSTRUMENTAL RATIONALITY: A COCKTAIL OF POSITIVISTIC ASSUMPTIONS MIXED WITH A MYRIAD OF NEOLIBERAL AND NEOCONSERVATIVE POLITICS?

A central theme of the theory of communicative action is a distinction between two fundamental forms of discourse—communicative and strategic. Habermas thus seeks to redefine the opposition—inherited from the German sociologist Max Weber—regarding the interplay between the 'instrumental' rationality of technical means and the 'substantial' rationality of ultimate ends or values. The first form of rationality corresponds to the 'cognitive-instrumental rationality' as defined by empiricism in the sciences and is oriented toward rationality as technical mastery. The second is associated with the notion of communicative rationality. (Morrow & Torres[7])

We have argued elsewhere that:

Positivism in the 19th century emerged as a position that stressed the unity of the logic of science; consequently, there was no basis for a methodological differentiation between the natural and the social sciences. Classic positivists defended the natural scientific model of causality and invariant laws as the logical basis of all inquiry.[8]

Positivistic notions of knowledge are built on a growing accumulation of facts, rather than a perception of the world characterized by discontinuities and small results with gradual consequences. Another disputable aspect of positivistic research is the notion of ownership of knowledge, which results from research being commissioned and subsidized by organizations (national and international) that retain control over the results. A third important assumption is that one could easily differentiated between doxa and episteme, and hence one could easily select empirical facts that are self-evident and differentiated from values. Value-free research, the neutrality and apoliticity of the researcher, and the possibility to measure, represent, and analyze every inch of human actions with a value-free methodology constitute a subset of epistemological premises of positivism.

It could be argued that some varieties of positivism are the dominant paradigm in the majority of financially driven research sponsored by the main players in education and social sciences (for instance, National Science Foundation, Department of Education, World Bank, some key foundations, etc). The successful projects are predicated on acceptable positivistic, rational choice theory, possessive individualistic accounts of human behavior, and social change akin to what I would like to term the *dominant neoliberal agenda* for globalization in K-12 schools and universities worldwide.

I have argued in Part I of this book that this agenda includes a drive toward privatization and decentralization of public forms of education, a movement toward educational standards, a strong emphasis on testing, and a focus on accountability. Specific to higher education, neoliberal versions of globalization suggest reforms for universities in four primary areas: efficiency and accountability, accreditation and universality, international competitiveness, and privatization.

These reforms, associated with international competitiveness, could be described as "competition-based reforms." These reforms are actively resisted in some countries by higher education professoriate, teachers unions, teachers, parents, students, and social movements. Indeed, globalization has had a major impact on education since international institutions have promoted finance-driven reforms, which eventually clash with the possibility of equity-driven reforms in many countries.

Therefore, the question is, to what extent globalization as competition-based reform has conspired against politics of inclusion, equality, and equity in some societies. Moreover, those people who begin from a weak position in the spheres of knowledge, skills, access to goods and services, or control over resources, will find that, left to themselves in the open market, their situation will likely deteriorate even further.

There are, to be sure, differential processes of implementation and adaptations of these financially driven, "competition-based" educational reforms in different countries. Differences depend on the history of each educational system, the type of government currently in power, and the role of teachers' unions and professional organizations, etc. Yet, not only is the implementation or the adoption of these reforms occurring, but a growing resistance to globalization at several levels is taking place as well.

Resistance, controversies, contradictions, and even activist confrontation to what is perceived as top-down imposed educational reforms through globalization policies and priorities, take place in diverse domains, including curriculum and instruction, teacher training, and school governance. This resistance is reflected in public debates about school reform as well.

Yet, a central focus of these debates will be on the specific cultural values that need to be preserved in each nation-state in terms of citizenship-building in the face of the prevailing cultural globalization through mass media and the trends of competition-based, financially driven educational reforms.

The main purpose of this chapter is not to examine and criticize those reforms. This has have been done elsewhere (for instance Apple, 2003; Torres, 2002). In this chapter, I simply aim to offer a set of arguments defending the framework of Critical Social Theory as a timely and energetic legacy that may help teachers, practitioners, researchers, policy activists, parents, and students to resist top-down globalization processes, challenging the key tenets of positivism[9] in social sciences and education. Critical Social Theory will help advancing a clearer and more compelling agenda for social research based on constructivism. The next section offers constructivism as a precondition to understanding the critique of Critical Social Theory , a strong challenger of positivism. Given the constraints of space, a few key central tenets of constructivism as an epistemological and methodological alternative will be examined.

IS CONSTRUCTIVISM AN ALTERNATIVE?[10]

> . . . possessing power inevitably corrupts the free exercise of reason.
>
> —Immanuel Kant, *Scriti Politici*

The polar opposite of positivism is a constructivist model of social science, reflecting a strong vision in which reality appears as a social construction, the product of discontinuities and unpredictable effects. Learners in the view of constructivists actively participate in learning, a notion that applies to the most elementary forms of learning and the most advance forms of research. Viewing all knowledge and learning as a social activity does not necessarily mean, as some postmodernists would argue, that we cannot potentially represent reality, but it does imply that we must acknowledge the diversity of perspectives involved in the formation of a community and a community of inquirers and teachers in particular. Abandoning the "quest for certainty" does not require abandoning the search for knowledge.

Methodological pluralism follows from a constructivist conception of scientific knowledge. This does not mean so much that "anything goes," but that we must acknowledge that there are diverse logics in use that make up inquiry. Accordingly, the key issue for policy research is the development of coherent research designs that link theory and research techniques appropriate to the questions asked and the problems to be solved.

A third premise, in stark contrast to positivism, is that knowledge cannot be separate from meaning and value, therefore education is necessarily a moral enterprise (Torres, 1998a). But in a culturally diverse society, this does not imply an absolute moral code, as opposed to procedural principles for guiding ethical thinking and action. In the context of education and the ethics of caring justice and individual responsibility are central principles of moral action that should complement each other.

As feminist theorists have reminded us, the nurturing principle of caring is at the heart of all learning as an interactive process that must respect the dignity of others. In the context of male-dominated culture, an ethics of caring can only emerge through a feminist approach providing the foundations for change. Feminist scholars have argued that the male experience is overwhelmingly reflected in education, and more generally, in public policy. We need to take very seriously the culture of "otherness," specifically women's culture and the cultures of "minorities" in schools, broadening the perspectives of citizenship education to include responsible and mutually respectful behavior in the domestic unit—the family—and in interpersonal relationships in society at large. Further, principles of social justice provide rational grounds for justifying criticism of social relations that undermine caring and the equitable fulfillment of human needs. Lastly, a notion of individual responsibility is central for the constitution of morality and ethics in education.

Learning is also an interactive process that should be organized around dialogical principles. Though not necessarily undermining the importance of intellectual authority and leadership, dialogical principles as predicated by John Dewey and Paulo Freire, among others, pose the question of the education of the educators and researchers and the need for reflexivity about what is to be taught, and what are the social uses of research. This reflexivity also calls into question the location of the researcher and the nature of her or his voice *vis a vis* his or her race, class, gender, religious commitments, sexual orientation, regionalism, nationalism, ideology, politics, and other important dimensions and dynamics in the constitution of identities, social agency, and social action.

Finally, constructivists recognized that research and education are socially and historically situated activities in institutions that are constrained and enabled by the power relations in the society around them. For this reason, an understanding of the role of expert knowledge, research, and education should be considered from the political sociology of education, paying attention to the relationships of the ideals and values embodied in researchers and research practices that seek to inform and guide educational policies. A fundamental legacy for the development of a political sociology of education is Critical Social Theory, to which I now turn my attention.

CRITICAL SOCIAL THEORY: A PORTRAIT

> I don't believe that we can change moral intuitions except as educators—that is, not as theoreticians and not as writers.
>
> —Jürgen Habermas, *Autonomy and Solidarity*, 1992: 202

> The thinker as lifestyle, as vision, as expressive self-portrait is no longer possible. I am not a producer of a Weltanschauung; I would really like to produce a few small truths, not the one big one.
>
> —Jürgen Habermas, *Autonomy and Solidarity*, 1992: 128

Unlike positivism, and beyond the analytical power of hermeneutics, a critical social science presupposes a kind of 'quasi-causal' structural analysis of

> depth interpretation" that illuminates the constraining and enabling effects of material (and institutional) realities ... but to be translated into practice this analytic knowledge must be rooted in the felt needs and sufferings of a group of people even though a great deal of what people do to one another is not the result of conscious knowledge and choice. [11]

The term *Critical Social Theory* is employed here following the tradition of the Frankfurt School, and particularly the work of Herbert Marcuse and his interpretation of the political and social philosophy of Hegel and Marx. Discussing the contribution of G.W.F. Hegel to social theory, Marcuse argued that:

> Hegel's system brings to a close the entire epoch in modern philosophy that had begun with Descartes and had embodied the basic ideas of modern society. Hegel was the last to interpret the world as reason, subjecting nature and history alike to the standards of thought and freedom. At the same time, he recognized the social and political order men had achieved as the basis on which reason had to be realized. His system brought philosophy to the threshold of its negation and thus constituted the sole link between the old and the new form of Critical Social Theory, between philosophy and social theory. [12]

Marcuse is right when he argues that determinate negation in Hegelian analysis lies in Marx's foundations when he advocates, in Lenin's words, the "merciless criticism of everything existing." What is the role of determinate negation in this process? As Smith explains:

> The logic of "determinate negation" is the principle of development which exhibits the movement from one category or form of consciousness to another. It constitutes a method for moving from one stage to another that is not externally imposed. . . . The logic of determinate negation has both a critical and a constructive aspect. It is critical because it does not merely accept what a body of thought, a philosophical system, or even an entire culture says about itself, but is concerned to confront that thought, system, or culture with its own internal tensions, incoherences, and anomalies. It is constructive because out of this negation or confrontation we are able to arrive at ever more complete, comprehensive, and coherent bodies of propositions and forms of life. [13]

This notion of negative philosophy is intimately associated with the notion of negation of negation in dialectics, and to the concept of determinate negation developed by Hegel and later transformed by Marx in *Das Kapital*. As I have argued elsewhere following Marcuse's analysis, [14] Hegelian dialectic is the rational construction of reality by which the subject assimilates his or her vital experience in an ongoing fashion until it finds itself again through the positivity of the determinate negation. Hegel foresaw that the subject would not only appropriate things (basic property), but that it was trying to appropriate the subjects as well (the struggle of the opposed consciousnesses); when the conflict of the two self-consciousnesses was brought to bear (that of each consciousness that had gone out of itself and was for itself), both fighting to appropriate the same good, a road toward a solution was being established. This road was the pact, a pact in which one of the two consciousnesses submitted to the other so as not to die. In this way, there came to light an independent consciousness and a dependent consciousness (dependent on the first one); in classical terms, the master (lord) and the slave (servant).

This notion of 'determinate negation' has become a centerpiece of early Critical Social Theory. Certainly, Herbert Marcuse draws from this notion of "determinate negation" when he speaks of the power of negative reason, and how that power is being obliterated in the context of authoritarian industrial societies.[15] Therefore, the rational nucleus of Hegelian dialectic is the notion of positivity of the determinate negation. For Hegel, self-consciousness tended to negate the actual forms that it would find along its way (as a notion and not the truth of thing-hood) in search of the emergence of the imminent unfolding of the Mind (which is its very self), present in daily life. This negation is denominated the positivity of the "determinate negation." History would thus be the road of the Mind, wholly self-conscious, which identifies with the totality of the historical process, whereas this historical process, in its logic, is nothing more than the manifestation—in itself already ahistorical—of imminent life at the historical unfolding of the Mind. The philosophizing consciousness (or the Mind) upon determinately negating the objects that confront it, with the aim of clearing a path on the road of rationality, in reality will be constructing an infinite totality, which is nothing more than its own life.

It is in Hegel that Marx found the substantial premises for the elaboration of his dialectical–historical philosophy, and the basic concepts that he cleverly employed to study the relationships between and among human beings and historically constituted structures. In so doing, Marx challenges the traditional epistemology in the subject–object relation, drawing from the Hegelian premise that material reality is a concrete totality constituted through social antagonisms. Within this Hegelian–Marxist framework that underpins the work of Critical Social Theory, the concept of labor is posited as determining the development of consciousness because human beings transform (and appropriate the fruits of) nature through their labor. This notion, in turn, is a central Hegelian contribution to Marx, particularly Hegel's suggestion that the opposition of consciousnesses is the result of the confrontation resulting from the desire of ego to appropriate things and even consciousness itself.

Marcuse argues that:

> The traditional epistemological antagonism between subject (consciousness) and object, Hegel makes into a reflection of a definite historical antagonism. The object first appears as an object of desire, something to be worked up and appropriated in order to satisfy a human want. In the course of the appropriation, the object becomes manifest as the "otherness" of man. [16]

This Hegelian premise is taken up by Marx who would argue that:

... the realization of labor appears as negation to such an extent that the worker is negated to the point of starvation. The objectification appears as a loss of the objects to such an extent that the worker is deprived of the most necessary objects of life and labor. Moreover, labor itself becomes an object of which he can make himself master only by the greatest effort and with incalculable interruption. Appropriation of the object appears as alienation to such an extent that the more objects the worker produces the less he possesses and the more he comes under the sway of his product, of capital.[17]

Hence, Marcuse's argument is that Marx found in Hegel's premises the foundations for his philosophy of history which challenged relativism and positivism alike.[18] Marcuse sees the rise of modern social theory in the link established by Hegel between philosophy and social theory. The post-Hegelian philosophical thought was dominated by positivism (or the positive philosophy in Marcuse's terminology), until Marx managed to deconstruct Hegel's philosophy of history, philosophy of rights, and dialectics, establishing the foundations of a negative philosophy:

> Hegel's critical and rational standards, and especially his dialectics, had to come into conflict with the prevailing social reality. For this reason, his system could well be called a *negative philosophy*, the name given to it by its contemporary opponents. To counteract its destructive tendencies, there arose, in the decade following Hegel's death, a positive philosophy[19] which undertook to subordinate reason to the authority of established fact. The struggle that developed between the negative and the positive philosophy offers ... many clues for understanding the rise of modern social theory in Europe.[20]

In short, Critical Social Theory appears as a negative philosophy not only because it challenges the tenets of the philosophy of positivism (a positive philosophy), but because, as it will be argued independently from Critical Social Theory by the Italian Marxist Antonio Gramsci, the theory helps to deconstruct the premises of common sense as contradictory and building hegemony. Or as Horkheimer puts it:

> Among the vast majority of the ruled there is the unconscious fear that theoretical thinking might show their painfully won adaptation to reality to be perverse and unnecessary.[21]

CRITICAL SOCIAL THEORY AND NEO-MARXISM

"The master-slave relationship, regardless of how colorful its disguise, dehumanizes the slave and the master. From an ethical point of view, and as the radical importance of ethics only grows, both the dominator and dominated are dehumanized."

—Paulo Freire, *Letters to Cristina*, 1996: 180.

The connections between the original brand of Critical Social Theory that inspired the origins of the Frankfurt School and its many associates (Walter Benjamin, Adorno, Max Horkheimer, Eric Fromm, Herbert Marcuse, and most importantly for education, Karl Manheim), and the original production of Marxism, built on three theoretical traditions (e.g., British Political Economy, German Philosophy, and French Socialism), is well documented and needs no further analysis. What is important, however, is to link the developments of the original Critical Social Theory with recent social theory as elaborated in the work of Jürgen Habermas or Claus Offe, and thus to relate Critical Social Theory to Neo-Marxism and the various forms of Critical Pedagogy.[22]

A central tenet of Critical Social Theory is Marx's analysis of the social production of material and symbolic life. Marx argued that:

In the social production which men carry on they enter into definitive relations that are indispensable and independent of their will; these relations of production correspond to a definite stage of development of their material forces of production. The sum total of these relations of production constitute the economic structure of society—the real foundation, on which rises the legal and political superstructure and to which correspond definite forms of social consciousness. The mode of production in material life determines the social, political and intellectual life in general. It is not the consciousness of men that determines their being, but, on the contrary, their social being that determines their consciousness.[23]

Yet, for Critical Social Theory, culture—as defined in the work of Gramsci and a host of Neo-Marxists writers—plays a central role in the production of hegemony and common sense interpretations of everyday life. The notion of negation and criticism implies the presumption that, in Ricoeur's hermeneutical analysis, all cultural relationships involve subtle codes of domination and discrimination.[24] The state appears as a site for contradictions and contested terrain, and therefore changes in the political alliances controlling the states are central for Neo-Marxist analysis.[25] The role of theories of the state must therefore be brought to the forefront of the debate.[26] The concepts of contradiction, dialectics, exploitation, domination, and legitimation are pivotal in the arsenal of Critical Social Theory and Neo-Marxism. The most recent theoretical developments have pushed the limits of original analyses based mostly on rigid notions of class as the ultimate determinant of collective social behavior, making the concept of class analytically compatible with (but not subordinated to) processes of discrimination and exploitation based on other key dimensions of human life, most prominently race, ethnicity, and gender relationships.

Critical Social Theory, however, has been mostly a tool for analysis and criticism as opposed to an attempt to undertake a journey in the realms of prophetism and utopia. Critical Social Theory has not tried to delineate the future developments of human interactions that it may deem most relevant for empowerment and liberation, which are indeed seen as the ultimate goals of any human experience, including scientific work. The role of socialism and the importance of the proletariat as the class that will eliminate all classes have been drastically tempered, if not simply abandoned, as a political program by many people who work closely with the Critical Social Theory tradition, but have decreed that Marxism, for all practical and theoretical purposes, is dead.[27] Finally, while not a monolithic approach, Neo-Marxist and Critical Social Theory perspectives include a call for democratic renewal, highlighting the importance of emancipatory social movements to democracy in contemporary capitalist societies.

THE NOTION OF 'CRITICAL' IN CRITICAL SOCIAL THEORY: AN INTELLECTUAL RESEARCH PROGRAM?

> Freedom needs authority to become free. It is a paradox but it is true. The question nevertheless is for authority to know that it has its authority in the freedom of others, and if the authority denies this freedom and cuts off this relationship, this founding relationship with freedom, I think that it is no longer authority but has become authoritarianism.
>
> —Paulo Freire, in Ira Shor and Paulo Freire,
> *A Pedagogy of Liberation: Dialogues on*
> *Transforming Education*, 1987: 91.

What is the meaning and nature of the concept of *critical* in Critical Social Theory? Canadian Critical Theorist, Raymond Morrow, offers an insightful set of distinctions when he argues that:

> The term *critical* itself, in the context of "Critical Social Theory" has a range of meanings not apparent in common sense where critique implies negative evaluations. This is, to be sure, one sense of critique in Critical Social Theory, given its concern with unveiling ideological mystifications in social relations; but another even more fundamental connotation is methodological, given a concern with critique as involving establishing the presuppositions of approaches to the nature of reality, knowledge, and explanation; yet another dimension of critique is

associated with the self-reflexivity of the investigator and the linguistic basis of representation (Morrow with Brown, 1994: 7).

Following Morrow's contribution, I would like to argue that, as a research program, Critical Social Theory implies several dimensions. It is a *human science,* hence providing a humanistic, anti-positivist approach to social theory. It is a *historical science of society,* hence it is a form of historical sociology. Finally, it is a *sociocultural critique* that is concerned with normative theory—that is, a

> theory about values and what ought to be. Critical imagination is required to avoid identifying where we live here and now as somehow cast in stone by natural laws.[28]

Yet, there is no singular Critical Social Theory, as Douglas Kellner has forcefully argued in his comprehensive study of the critical tradition initiated by the Frankfurt School.[29] A definitive feature of this theoretical cluster and research program is its interdisciplinary nature, defying the logic of separate disciplines analyzing discrete objects of study:

> Critical Social Theory has refused to situate itself within an arbitrary or conventional division of labor. It thus traverses and undermines boundaries between competing disciplines, and stresses interconnections between philosophy, economics and policies, and culture and society[30]

Another important insight from Kellner's analysis is the notion that Critical Social Theory attempts a synthesis that, as a research program, can only be accomplished through collective groups of intellectuals aiming at social transformation:

> [A Critical Social Theory] project requires a collective, supradisciplinary synthesis of philosophy, the science and politics, in which critical social theory is produced by groups of theorists and scientists from various disciplines working together to produce a Critical Social Theory of the present age aimed at radical social-political transformation.[31]

This notion of Critical Social Theory has serious implications for the role of intellectuals in contemporary capitalist societies, for the role of social theory in the context of debates about modernism and postmodernism, and for the role that education, and particularly the political sociology of education, may play.

For the Critical Social Theory tradition, theory cannot be easily separated from practice. Hence, as discussed below, a political sociology of education should improve not only the understanding of social reality (i.e., Enlightenment) or improve the epistemological, logical, and analytical perspectives of meta-theory, theory, and empirical research, (i.e., theorizing), but should also contribute to the improvement of the practice of policy makers, policy brokers, and policy constituencies, and the cognitive and non-cognitive outcomes of the process of teaching and learning. A byproduct of this discussion is the role of intellectuals employing Critical Social Theory as opposed to liberal, neoliberal, and neoconservative intellectuals employing mainstream theories.

THE ROLE OF CRITICAL INTELLECTUALS IN CRITICAL SOCIAL THEORY: CONCLUSION

> There exist an international citizenship that has its rights and its duties, and that obliges one to speak out against every abuse of power, whoever the author, whoever the victim.
>
> —Foucault, M. *Essential Works of Foucault*, volume 3, *Power*, 2000: 474

The statement by Foucault that opens this section invites us to think what is the role of critical intellectuals. The answer from the perspective of Critical Social Theory seems to be self-evident: to be the critics of the system following the logic of determinate negation, but not a critic who is necessarily intransigent or intolerant by definition. Rather, to be one who is able to offer to society, like a mirror, the critical aspects that need to be considered in dealing with mechanisms of sociability, production, and political exchanges. Indeed, universities, as a place inhabited by intellectuals and not only by technocrats, have a role to play in developing critical modes of thinking for society. This implies, additionally, a critique of the commodification of human relations, and in the context of universities themselves, a critique of the corporatization of academic institutions as is currently outlined by the graduate employee unionization movement in the United States.[32]

A third element is that Critical Social Theory assumes that a central role of intellectuals is to create a social imaginary—and hence, Gramsci's hypotheses about organic and traditional intellectuals (Morrow and Torres, 1991). The creation of social imaginary implies, for critical intellectuals, a moral responsibility and a political commitment: a moral responsibility to imagine social scenarios where people can deliberate and construct mechanisms of participation, which may expand the workings of democracy and a political commitment to create a sphere of public debate, as suggested by Habermas; an autonomous sphere of public deliberation, which is neither controlled by the market nor controlled by the state.

What else can be said about the role of intellectuals in the critical modernist tradition? Gramsci proposed a forceful hypothesis when he argued that everybody has the capacity to do intellectual work, but only a few recognize it, and/or work in intellectual professions. Hence, two key elements emerge from Gramsci's suggestion. First, that intellectual work is not only a trade, a set of techniques, or a profession, but the capacity to realize refined analysis, which leads to praxis and social transformation. Second, a critical intellectual in the tradition of critical modernism is one who is able not only to teach but also to learn from the people, from the popular sectors. Paraphrasing Mao Tse Tung, a critical intellectual is one who is also able to capture the collective imagination of the people, in all its disorganized richness and insightfulness, and is able to return this knowledge back to the people, but this time in a more systematic and organized fashion. Therefore, the very same producers of the knowledge are be able to appraise, reinterpret, and rethink their own knowledge and insights, both conceptually and practically.

The production of knowledge in the human sciences is a process that involves a great deal of persuasion. Intellectuals are always trying to persuade each other, trying to show that they have a better explanation and a more powerful, far-reaching, and/or complete analysis than a previous or competing one. From a constructivist perspective however, critical intellectuals are convinced that there is never a perfect or comprehensive interpretation or understanding, nor a conclusive analysis that cannot be challenged or subject to debate and criticism. Perhaps the best way to put it is the notion of Hegelian "Aufhebung": Knowledge creation is always the negation on the previous negation, the criticism of previous knowledge, which, in and by itself, is a criticism of previous knowledge and so forth.

Hence, assuming this notion of "Aufhebung" invites a sense of humility and humbleness to intellectual work. Intellectuals always work with knowledge produced by someone else—not only individuals but collectives. Critical intellectuals see their work as always provisory and limited. They cannot be detached clinicians offering "objective" advice. While intellectual work is seen by conventional wisdom as eminently individual, or the work of a team of individuals who share similar analytical, theoretical, and methodological premises, for critical intellectuals it is collective work because it always draws from previous knowledge, and the criticism of previous knowledge. Therefore, the notion of learning is as important as the notion of teaching in knowledge construction.

Critical intellectuals assume an agonic perspective in knowledge production. Assuming that no intellectual work can provide a definitive answer to virtually any domain or problem of the human sciences, critical intellectuals cannot, for moral and political reasons, give up continuing the process of mutual persuasion, even if their intellectual product may be short lived. Marcuse offers a compelling argument to justify the moral dimensions of the work of critical intellectuals. Speaking, perhaps for the last time to his disciple, Jürgen Habermas, he said, "Look, I know wherein our most basic value judgment are rooted—in compassion, in our sense for the suffering of others."[33]

In political terms, a critical intellectual pays as much attention to the process as it does to the product of intellectual work—both as individual and collective endeavors. In so doing, critical modernist intellectuals remain key facilitators of intellectual exchanges in the production of collective symbolism and rituals. They remain keys to the facilitation of the creation of spaces for public conversation, as Paulo Freire exemplified throughout his own life. A few years ago, I was interviewing Freire and I asked him what he would like his legacy to be. He answered that when he died, he would like people to say of him: "Paulo Freire lived, loved, and wanted to know." (See Carlos A. Torres, *Learning the World.* Paulo Freire conversation with Carlos Alberto Torres ACCESS Network [Caudar Public Television] Education, Alberta, Canada, October 1990, videotape). Freire, in his poetic style, provided a simple and yet powerful message about the role of critical intellectuals. For Freire, critical intellectuals should live their own ideas passionately, building spaces of deliberation and tolerance in their quest for knowledge and empowerment. They love what they do, and those with whom they interact. Love, then, becomes another central element in the political project of intellectuals agonizing in producing knowledge for empowerment and liberation.

Finally, it is their love for knowledge itself that makes them sensitive to the popular knowledge and common sense. Following Gramsci, critical intellectuals know that common sense has always had a nucleus of "good sense." From this "good sense" of the common sense, critical intellectuals can develop a criticism of conventional wisdom, knowledge, and practices. In educational policy and planning, this "good sense" could be a starting point for a critique of instrumental rationalization. In this context, critical intellectuals may resort to a political sociology of education to understand educational policy formation.[34]

The lessons of Critical Social Theory for education are clear, and need to be remembered: politics and education intersect continually—there is an inherent politicity of education. Power plays a major role in configuring schooling and social reproduction. Social change cannot be simply articulated as social engineering from the calm environment of the research laboratory. Social change needs to be forged in negotiations, compromise, but also fighting in the political system. It needs to be struggled over in the streets with the social movements; to be conquered in the schools struggling against bureaucratic and authoritarian behavior, defying the growing corporatization of educational institutions, particularly in higher education, and striving to implement substantive rationality through communicative dialogue; and to be achieved even in the cozy and joyful environment of our gatherings with our family and friends. Dialogue and reason cannot take vacations if one pursues the dream of social justice, education, and peace.

Curiously enough, the current process of globalization—if it is not simply understood as globalization from above as a neoliberal imprint—could contribute as globalization from below, to challenge some of the principles neglecting human rights and freedom in capitalist societies, henceforth enhancing the chances for cosmopolitan democracies and radical educational reform. Critical Social Theory has a major role to play to achieve those goals.

7 Globalization, Education, and Transformative Social Justice Learning
A Preliminary Draft of a Theory of Marginality[1]

INTRODUCTION

> The only absolutely certain thing is the future, since the past is constantly changing.[2]

In this book, I have defended the idea that there are many definitions of globalization, or perhaps more accurately, there are many globalizations. For example, globalization has been defined as:

> the intensification of worldwide social relations which link distant localities in such a way that local happenings are shaped by events occurring many miles away and vice versa. [3]

Another view sees globalization as:

> a feature of late capitalism, or the condition of postmodernity, and, more important . . . the emergence of a world system driven in large part by a global capitalist economy. [4]

Others see globalization as the transformation of time and space in which complex interactions and exchanges once impossible become everyday activities.[5] Still others see globalization as an assault on traditional notions of society and the nation-state whereby the very nature of citizenship and social change is dramatically altered.[6]

In the "longue duree," as Braudel would have put it, globalization processes, as historical facts have been part of the human adventure almost since its beginnings. The expansion of the Greek culture and the Roman Empire, the dissemination of the main staples that people grow and consume, which have been spread by consumption patterns of specific cultural groups, or the growth and spread of the world's great religions, are representative of different types of globalization in their own right. The globalizations of AIDS and SARS could be considered contemporary manifestations of the great European plague.

In short, with globalization we are witnessing a social phenomenon that is neither new nor unique in the way it has percolated social institutions and cultures in the world. Some of the work of Immanuel Wallerstein on world systems and the transformation of the Mediterranean countries alongside the transformation of capitalism and its impact in the globe detail processes of globalization that can be traced back centuries.[7] What is new, perhaps, in this new wave of globalization is that it entails a simultaneous change in the dynamics by which capital, labor, and technology expand across borders with a pace and intensity never seen before, impacting, particularly the realm of culture. With this brief background, it will be important to focus on the many faces of globalization from a political economy perspective, and to outline some of the implications for education. I will not develop in this chapter a substantive analysis of the implications of globalization for culture and mass media, which has been articulated exceedingly well by Raymond Morrow.[8]

What I believe is important is how we can confront the project and dynamics of the neoliberal globalization. To this extent, the work of Paulo Freire, and the possibilities of transformative social justice learning as a theory of marginality, open important avenues for thinking, theorizing, and the praxis of social transformation.

PAULO FREIRE, DEMOCRACY, AND CITIZENSHIP: KEY PRINCIPLES

Freire addresses a serious dilemma of democracy, the constitution of democratic citizenship. In the sixties, he suggested a model of diversity and crossing borders in education that became a central tenet in the discussion of transformative social justice learning. As a social, political, and pedagogical practice, transformative social justice learning will take place when people reach a deeper, richer, more textured understanding of themselves and of their world, and when they are prepared to act upon this new understanding. Based on the normative assumption of critical theory that most social exchanges involve a relationship of domination, and that language constitutes identities, from a meaning-making or symbolic perspective, transformative social justice learning attempts to recreate various theoretical contexts for the examination of rituals, myths, icons, totems, symbols, and taboos in education and society, seeking to understand and transform social agency and structures. It is imperative, then, to start addressing the question of democratic dilemmas.

DEMOCRATIC DILEMMAS

Freire addresses a serious dilemma of democracy, the constitution of a democratic citizenship. In the sixties—quite early compared with the postmodernist preoccupations of the eighties—he advanced the question of diversity and border crossing in education, central tenets of transformative social justice learning. Freire taught us that domination, aggression, and violence are intrinsic parts of human and social life. Freire also argued that few human encounters are extent of one type of oppression or another; by virtue of race, ethnicity, class, and gender, people tend to be victims or perpetrators of oppression. Thus, for Freire, sexism, racism, and class exploitation are the most salient forms of domination. Yet, exploitation and domination exist on other grounds, including religious beliefs, political affiliation, national origin, age, size, and physical and intellectual abilities to name just a few. [9]

Starting from a psychology of oppression influenced by psychotherapists like Freud, Jung, Adler, Fanon, and Fromm, Freire developed a pedagogy of the oppressed. In the spirit of the Enlightenment, he believed in education as a means to improve the human condition, confronting the effects of a psychology and a sociology of oppression, contributing ultimately to what Freire considered the ontological vocation of the human race: humanization. In the introduction to his highly acclaimed *Pedagogy of the Oppressed*, Freire states, "From these pages I hope it is clear my trust in the people, my faith in men and women, and my faith in the creation of a world in which it will be easier to love."[10]

Freire was known as a philosopher and a theoretician of education in the critical perspective; an intellectual who never separated theory from practice. In *Politics and Education* he forcefully stated that "Authoritarism is like necrophilia, while a coherent democratic project is biophilia."[11] It is from this epistemological standpoint that Freire's contribution resonates as the basic foundation for transformative social justice learning. The notion of democracy entails the notion of a democratic citizenship in which agents are active participants in the democratic process, able to choose their representatives as well as to monitor their performance. These are not only political but also pedagogical practices because the construction of the democratic citizen implies the construction of a pedagogic subject. Individuals are not, by nature themselves, ready to participate in politics. They have to be educated in democratic politics in a number of ways, including normative grounding, ethical behavior, knowledge of the democratic process, and technical performance. The construction of the pedagogic subject is a central conceptual problem, a dilemma of democracy. To put it simply: democracy implies a process of participation where all are considered equal. However, education involves a process whereby the 'immature' are brought in to identify with the principles and life forms of the "mature" members of society.

Thus, the process of construction of the democratic pedagogic subject is a process of cultural nurturing, involving cultivating principles of pedagogic and democratic socialization in subjects who are neither *tabula rasa* in cognitive or ethical terms, nor fully equipped for the exercise of their democratic rights and obligations.[12] Yet, in the construction of modern polities, the constitution of a pedagogical democratic subject is predicated on grounds that are, paradoxically, a precondition but also the result of previous experiences and policies of national solidarity (including citizenship, competence-building, and collaboration).[13]

A second major contribution of Freire's is his thesis, advanced in *Pedagogy of the Oppressed* and reiterated in countless writings, that the pedagogical subjects of the educational process are not homogeneous citizens but culturally diverse individuals. From his notion of cultural diversity, he identified the notion of crossing borders in education, suggesting that there is an ethical imperative to cross borders if we attempt to educate for empowerment and not for oppression. Crossing the lines of difference is, indeed, a central dilemma of transformative social justice learning.

TRANSFORMATIVE SOCIAL JUSTICE LEARNING AND A PRELIMINARY DRAFT OF A THEORY OF MARGINALITY

> Tolerance does not abdicate your dreams for which you intransigently struggle, but respects those dreams that are different from yours. For me, at the political level, tolerance is wisdom or the virtue of cohabiting with the different in order to argue with the antagonistic. In this way, it is a revolutionary and not a liberal-conservative virtue.
>
> —Paulo Freire

Hopefully it is clear that to deal with all the faces of globalization outlined in this book and to analyze the implications for education is not an easy feat. Likewise, to explore the limits and possibilities of a model of transformative social justice learning in the context of globalization and the challenges to education require not only acumen, but also theoretical sophistication and steel political will. My purpose in this concluding section is to outline, in preliminary form, a theory of marginality.

We have defined transformative social justice learning as a social construct reflecting a social, political, and pedagogical practice that will take place when people reach a deeper, richer, more textured, and nuanced understanding of themselves and their world. Not in vain, Freire always advocated the simultaneous reading of the world and of the word. Based on a key assumption of critical theory—that all social relationships involve a relationship of domination, and that language constitutes identities—transformative social justice learning, from a meaning-making or symbolic perspective, is an attempt to recreate the various theoretical contexts for the examination of rituals, myths, icons, totems, symbols, and taboos in education and society; an examination of the uneasy dialectic between agency and structure, moving forward a process of transformation. From a sociological perspective, transformative social justice learning entails an examination of systems, organizational processes, institutional dynamics, rules, mores, and regulations, including prevailing traditions and customs, i.e., key structures that, by definition, reflect human interest.

In examining the implications of globalization for education, how can we take advantage of transformative social justice learning as a methodology and theory of social transformation? Let me be bold: one may argue that this model of transformative social justice learning is a marginal social construct in the context of contemporary social politics. Moreover, those who embrace and practice this approach are, by definition, marginal to the overall dynamics of institutional political struggle, and to the process of institutional development in academia and elsewhere. Hence, we may outline the principles of a theory of marginality.

Politically one may need to understand that marginality is not simply being an outsider, marginal to a core of practices, values, or institutions, but it constitutes a specific form of insertion in the context of the global debate, as well as the struggle for social justice. The notion of marginality thus became a central notion to pursue transformative social justice learning. We pursue this approach even if we know that we are marginal to the central concepts and practices of the liberal and conservative establishments (which seem to be, in education at least, poised to emphasize the need to improve cognitive learning through the movement of testing, accountability in schools, or to endorse a progressive process of privatization of public education).

Yet, the idea of marginality doesn't rest simply on notions of opposition or negativity against positivism, and positivity of the pedagogical, political, and epistemological models that predominate in academia and social life. We cannot accept our marginality predicated only on the difficulties that we face, or in the losses that we endure in this long haul, the long *duree* of social struggles. We shall also celebrate, within the notion of marginality, the different triumphs that we have in our struggles. That we cannot criticize without celebrating is a principle of marginality.

Marginality as a construct pays tribute to the Latin adagio *ad fontes*. The notion of marginality is predicated on resorting to historical nuanced analyses of the dynamics between social agencies and structures, and on a refined conceptual understanding that draws upon the strengths of Critical Social Theory (Morrow and Torres 1995). As such, the notion of marginality is both a model of advocacy with important normative implications and an analytical model with clear political objectives. Remember Freire's dictum: we teach against somebody and on behalf of somebody; we teach on behalf of some values or against some values. Thus the notion of the politicity of education that Freire defended throughout his life is a central tenet of marginality as an epistemological, political, and even spiritual position in education.

Marginality is an invitation to struggle in the long haul, linking theory and praxis, not only as an individual, but also as part and parcel of broader social movements. In so doing, a notion of marginality proclaims the need to hear the marginal voices, voices that reclaim their positioning in the debates, voices that need to be heard in the process of political deliberation. Thus marginality is a central concept in the notion of the public spheres as a theater of political deliberation, which is controlled neither by the state nor by the market. Therefore, reclaiming the transformative role of teachers as public intellectuals, and of teachers' unions and social movements in the context of defending public education as a foundation of the social democratic pact, is an imperative of the theory and practice of marginality in politics.

While being marginal invites us to speak in anger against oppressive living conditions, unethical behavior, corruption, violence, environmental degradation, inequality, and the like, anger itself could be made a political tool for social movements and individuals. However, one must be careful not to fall into the trap of self-victimization, always blaming someone else for your ills, failures, or sadness. With marginality comes a notion of individual responsibility that needs to be honored. Hence, marginality as a political and practical option draws on a model of spirituality that is clearly utopian and utopistic. It is utopian because, as many poets have suggested, utopia is like a distant horizon, a horizon that one wants to reach but never does. One walks two steps to reach it, and the horizon moves two steps farther. One walks two more steps, and the horizon moves two steps farther away. What, then, is the advantage of utopia as a political rationale and spiritual endeavor? It helps us to keep walking.

Marginality is also utopian in another sense of the word: in the prophetic biblical sense of utopia. The utopia of denouncing the causes of exploitation, oppression, and inequality while simultaneously announcing, not the coming of the Messiah, but the possibility of a better world, a world, in the words of Paulo Freire, in which it will be easier to love. As Freire said,

> The prophets are not men or women badly dressed, poorly groomed, unshaven and dirty, wearing baggy clothes and carrying a shepherd's staff. The prophets are those that submerge themselves in the waters of their culture, their history, and the history of the oppressed of their *pueblo*. Prophets are those who know their "here" and "now," and therefore they can not only foresee the future, but they can realize it."[14]

However, marginality as a political position draws not only on utopian premises but also on utopistic models. We want to examine the different alternative models of society—the utopistic models—as different social constructions that are emerging in contemplating the transformation of society, drawing from a perception of what a "good society" is. After all, even the notion of neoliberalism is a utopistic model, comparable for instance, to another utopistic model for a 'good society,' Leninism.

If, for conservatives, democracy is deliberate delusion and politics is the industry and the art of emasculating the truth, marginality may become both an antidote to the ills of democracy as spectacle and its nongovern-ability—recently exemplified in an action-hero celebrity replacing a career politician as governor of the richest state of the union—as well as a suggestive methodological approach based on the principle of uncertainty, so well developed by physicist and Nobel Prize Illya Prigigoni. A theory of marginality may help us to achieve what many scholars, including Morris Berman, so aptly termed the "re-enchantment of the world."

Part III

Biography as a Genre of Political Pedagogical Struggle

8 Education, Power, and Personal Biography

An Interview with Carlos Alberto Torres by Armando Alcántara Santuario[1]

Armando Alcántara (AA): First, I'd like to ask what have been the main topics that have occupied your attention in recent years? Your academic career begins in 1975 with your appointment as assistant professor in political philosophy at the University of El Salvador in Argentina. The following year you finished your first book on Paulo Freire, which was published in Mexico in 1978. The year 2000 marks your twenty-fifth anniversary as a professor and university investigator.

Carlos Alberto Torres (CAT): Twenty-five years of professional work in any sphere of human life is an invitation to reflection, not nostalgia, but to learn and to re-learn, as an intellectual committed to social change and emancipatory education, what I have accomplished as a professor and an investigator. In that spirit and with great appreciation for this opportunity to speak about my work, I have to say that I think it is impossible to design a research agenda by simply following the guidelines and regulations of the academy, or by following a precise plan sketched out beforehand in the calm of one's office, or by responding to the demands of social movements, political parties or public policy. A research agenda originates from a complex process that includes all of these things, where intellectual and political preferences are combined with the challenges and struggles of daily life and felicitous opportunities to learn more, in theoretical and empirical terms, by playing a part in an educational process or problem. As a single individual, it is difficult to carry out a research agenda that puts together theoretical, conceptual, empirical and normative efforts, either in the solitude of your own thoughts or by systematic application of scientific methods in the solitude of your fieldwork.

My agenda of investigation and educational practice has often been carried out in collaboration with colleagues of enormous human and intellectual worth who are also my friends and, in some cases, former students whom I had the opportunity to serve as professor and advisor. I would like to mention, in this regard, the works that I have written with Raymond Morrow, over a period of fifteen years of such close collaboration that, in matters of social theory, it is difficult to discern who has written what in some of our books and a number of research articles. I have also co-authored books with José Angel Pescador, Daniel Schugurensky, Adriana Puiggrós, Pilar O' Cadiz, Pía Wong, Robert Arnove, Ted Mitchell, Daniel A. Morales Gomez, Nick Burbules, Martin Carnoy, Henry Levin, Marcela Mollis, Jerry Kachur, Seewha Cho, Aurora Loyo, Julie Thompson, Moacir Gadotti, Karen McClafferty, Guillermo Gonzalez Rivera, and with you and Ricardo Pozas Horcasitas.

No doubt, a crucial point in my academic career was being hired, in March 1990, as a professor at the UCLA Graduate School of Education and Information Science. It gave me the opportunity to continue my investigations, under the rubric of Latin American education, to complete some projects I initiated in the 1970s and 1980s, and to start down new conceptual and empirical paths. UCLA has been an intellectually and emotionally inspiring place for me, as well as an absolutely remarkable political environment, which has given me constant material and practical support and allowed me to continue to struggle with work that sometimes generates contradictions and enormous difficulties.

It might be convenient to synthesize the general theme of my investigations around the relationship between education, power, and policy. This has been the directive thread of my work throughout these twenty-five years. This generic line of research takes the shape of three wide sub-themes, which I have explored in different books and research articles, and about which I have made countless presentations in international meetings and conferences. In the political sociology of education, it is necessary to understand why a specific educational policy begins, how it is created, planned, constructed, and implemented. What are the key ingredients and actors in its formulation and operationalization and what systemic, symbolic, historico-structural and organizational processes are involved in its inception, implementation, and evaluation?

A second general theme in my work these last twenty-five years is what were known, throughout the 1960s and 1970s, as characteristics of the dependent capitalist state in Latin America, specifically with respect to the formulation of educational policy. My specific concern in this regard was to gain an understanding of the state's nature and need for legitimation and to observe and analyze how its dependent character conditioned the nature of the formulation of educational policy, especially in the area of non-formal education. This second area, which includes my work in Mexico during the last part of the 1970s and my return there after getting my doctorate at Stanford in the beginning of the 1980s, was focused on the study of adult education. In this area, I tried to create what I call a "political sociology of non-formal education," which consumed most of the 1980s and terminated abruptly due to my disappointment with the lack of political commitment of most of the Latin American states, which paid lip service to adult education policy as one of the mechanisms of state legitimizing with no real intention to put it into effect. My disappointment was also due to the indisputable, empirically proven, fact that Latin American states have manipulated adult education policies to their benefit while ceasing to invest in adult education programs. There was also a long tradition of struggle and investment in education that affected important areas of public administration and that has been losing momentum for the last ten or fifteen years with the encroachment of neoliberalism.

A third topic which summarizes many of the investigations I made in these last two and a half decades has to do with alternatives developed in Latin America to combat the tendency of the state to use educational policy as what Habermas calls "compensatory legitimizing." Once I began to understand with greater clarity the relations between neo-Marxism, especially that of Gramsci, and the decisive contributions of critical theory, particularly those of Herbert Marcuse and Paulo Freire, I realized that these notions of compensatory legitimizing are crucial to understanding certain state practices. While searching for alternatives, I found that the influence of Paulo Freire's work on these topics has been very important. I have tried thus far to carry out a systematic analysis of one of the most original and creative thinkers Latin America, and particularly Brazil, has ever produced. As an intellectual and political philosopher of education, Freire offers an endless number of contributions to the region and the world at large and invites us to think about critical educational alternatives. *Pedagogy of the Oppressed* is one of the most important contributions to emancipative education as is his final legacy, a small, incisive and tremendously suggestive text about educational ethics, *Pedagogy of Autonomy*.

Freire's life-long study of how pedagogy impelled practices that can contribute either to oppression or to liberation culminates with a political strategy for the unfettered autonomy of the pedagogical subject in the context of a fully autonomous "citizen school." Paulo Freire's legacy of struggle is also that of popular education in Latin America, which has been a distinguished tradition in the region since the beginning of the twentieth century.

Applying the theories of the state to the field of education has given me room to initiate a systematic exploration of themes that appear in one of my most recent books, *Education, Democracy and Multiculturalism: Dilemmas of Citizenship in a Global World*, which is at this moment being translated into Spanish and will be published in Mexico by Siglo XXI Editors. In this new line of investigation, which will probably take another decade to complete, I attempt to take from the theory of the state and the analysis of the theory of globalization, aspects that have to do with the theory of citizenship, the theory of democracy, and nascent theories of multiculturalism, to offer a series of reflections on how multicultural, democratic citizenship can be established. This has been the main concern of my work for the last five years.

Along with this, as a professor specializing in Latin American education at UCLA, I have continued with more generic research into educational politics, lately concerning the relationship between teacher unions and state policy in six countries: Argentina, Mexico, Canada, the United States,

Japan, and Korea. Clearly a work of this scope, with fieldwork conducted in half a dozen distinct cultures (supported financially by the Soka Foundation of Japan, and the Pacific Rim Center of the University of California), is impossible without the collaboration of a group of talented investigators in comparative education, including Julie Thompson, Aurora Loyo, Marcela Mollis, Seehwa Cho, Jerry Kachur, Daniel Schugurensky, and Akio Nagao. After four years of work, we are currently completing a collective book about this international investigation into education, policy and the state on the so-called "Pacific Rim."

AA: Carlos, what do you see as the main contributions of Latin America to the discussion of educational problems in the international sphere?

CAT: That is a difficult question to answer since the contributions are of such quality and so varied that one runs the risk of omitting some of them. On the one hand, we have all the aspects related to social theory applied to different issues of culture, the symbolic phenomena and, of course, education. In Latin America we have seen the development, especially in the last thirty to thirty-five years, of liberation theology and the theory of dependency; we have also had all the developments of the philosophy of liberation and of course, popular education and Freire's pedagogy of the oppressed. I dare say that there has been a contribution not only to education but to the social sciences in general, which has burnished the development of the social sciences, both in Latin America and the world, from theories of decolonization to questions and debates on the role of race. Recently, the work of Néstor García Canclini on hybrid cultures, the Brazilian Roberto da Matta on issues of the quotidian, and a series of writings by other experts on the problematic of culture, lead me to believe that there is a theoretical wealth in Latin America that has deeply impacted intellectual work at a worldwide level. On the other hand, at the political level, the struggles against military dictatorship and in favor of human rights, have elevated the discussion to a higher level of responsibility and worldwide concern that perhaps, without the Mothers of the Plaza de Mayo in Argentina and the struggle against Pinochet in Chile, to mention only two very well-known and relevant cases, would not have been projected into the international arena, calling attention to the perennial quest for human rights and peace that has resulted in the granting of Nobel Peace Prizes to people like Pérez Esquivel, Rigoberta Menchú, and Oscar Arias.

At a more specific educational level, I believe that a second element has been the momentum provided by Paulo Freire who, in the second half of the twentieth century, became known as the finest thinker in educational philosophy, particularly in the political philosophy of education, since John Dewey. I believe that Paulo Freire is also a nerve center for two other topics, which are part of the logic of academic work that we have in Latin America and which are relatively different from those which exist elsewhere in the world. The first is our concern with epistemology. Without any doubt, in Latin America we think about education from an epistemological perspective, in a richer way than is thought elsewhere. On the other hand, I believe that in Latin America there is a certain spirit of comparative analysis, in the sense that structural historical analyses predominate. By their very nature, these comparative historical processes through time at a synchronic–diachronic level that has given rise to an extraordinarily rich training in the capacity to think about reality. It is for this reason that Latin Americans have an expression that is difficult to find in other intellectual spaces, which is the notion of "pensadores" (thinkers): Paulo Freire was a thinker. If you want to transform this term into more contemporary terminology, we are speaking of "public intellectuals." There are public intellectuals outside Latin America, for instance Noam Chomsky in the United States. But it is my impression that the comparative notion of public intellectuals and education predominates in Latin America, where practically every country has one or two public intellectuals of enormous scope, and that this has lent a tone and a level of intellectual hierarchy to the academic–political discussion that is not so easy to find in surroundings where positivist and empiricist thought prevails. It is also possible that, in comparatively apolitical surroundings, the logic of instrumental reason dictates practice, unmodified by the presence of political logic.

There are so many elements to your question. It also seems clear to me that Latin America has been one of the great laboratories for the establishment of the politics of privatization, and this is the part that pleases me least. I am not talking about vouchers, but about privatization in the sense of what are called "user fees," and other aspects tied to the notion of decentralization as part of the hegemonic agenda. Then too, the region has been a virtual laboratory for the mechanisms and models of structural adjustment, on whose impact it will be necessary to make a stricter evaluation in the long term. But Latin America, much more than Africa, Asia, and the Middle East, has been a territory where these types of models have been implemented in quite a radical manner, and with structural adjustments that have been rather brutal.

And finally, why not emphasize something fundamental, the normal school model? The concept was born in France but has bloomed in Latin America as an extraordinary ideology that drives teacher training and gives teachers a specific task, almost like that of a missionary. Despite all the weaknesses that this model possesses, it has been a central element in creating mechanisms for the training and qualification of teachers. It has also been crucial in creating a teacher workforce and in helping define the notion of "legitimate knowledge" and adopting curricular models that benefit it. What is more, in the twentieth century, the normal school model has been intimately tied to the very definition of schooling in Latin America. I believe that a more advanced argument could be made, and that one of its elements would be the idea of the liberal and democratic state that has impelled the formation of citizenship through education.

AA: Carlos, from what you have said in your previous answers and from what is known of your own work, you have a wealth of knowledge and a critical approach when it comes to Paulo Freire's work, which you have also helped introduce to the English-speaking world. We know that you had a very close relationship with him. How did your interest in education for liberation begin?

CAT: Well, anyone who knew Paulo Freire immediately discovered an extraordinary man: a human being with enormous dignity, a deeply charismatic and often prophetic force, and an individual who exemplified the best of Latin American oral culture. He tried to understand reality from the stimuli that it provided and his observational ability. And this ability in Paulo Freire was absolutely masterful. But there was also his ability to elaborate ideas, his constant reference to the epistemology of curiosity. All these elements magnetized anyone who knew Paulo Freire. But, in addition to his personality, his ethical perspective on the world, his impressive honesty, there was also what I would call his continual effort to attain ever greater levels of technical competence and intellectual rigor in anything he undertook, and the expectation that his collaborators would do the same.

I got acquainted with Paulo Freire the same way most of the intellectuals of my generation did: by reading *Education as the Practice of Freedom and Pedagogy of the Oppressed*, printed by Tierra Nueva, his first publisher, around 1973. I wrote my first book on Paulo Freire in 1975 at the urging of Julio Barreiro, who was Freire's publisher at that time and an extraordinarily lucid man, an Uruguayan professor well-trained in philosophy and living in Argentina due to the difficult circumstances through which the Uruguayan democracy was passing under military dictatorship. I wrote Paulo in Geneva and he answered, pre-technological man that he was, with a hand-written letter thanking me very much for the materials I had sent him, especially for an article, one of my first analyses of his work, published in the Brazilian journal *Sínteses*. I think the fact that it had been published in Portuguese must have meant a lot to him. In that article, I analyzed the major philosophical antecedents of Paulo's thought. He wrote, with his customary gentility, that the article had impressed him because it appeared to be an excellent interpretation of his work. That's how our relationship started, first in an epistolary way, and then face-to-face when I visited him in Brazil in the early 1980s. Over the years, we became very good friends. There was, I would say, a mutual affinity and an enormous respect, on my part, for someone who has been the "maestro" for generations of Latin American educators. I also wanted to know how Freire thought on his feet and this became apparent in our conversations over a twenty-year period. In 1986, the year his first wife Elza died, he invited me to dinner one night and said: "I am going to introduce you to one of my best friends, and I know that he will also become a great friend of yours." That night I met Moacir Gadotti with whom I created, along with Freire, Walter García, Francisco Gutiérrez and José Eustáquio Romão, the Paulo Freire Institute of São Paulo in 1991, of which I have the honor of being one of the founding directors. The PFI is also the present seat of the CLACSO

(Latin American Council of Social Sciences) Working Group on Education and Society that I serve as coordinator.

My first encounter with Moacir more than fifteen years ago introduced me to a man with a great sense of humanity and an exceptional intellectual lucidity. I have learned a lot from him, from Paulo Freire, and from the rest of the Institute's team, despite the twists and turns, tensions, labyrinths, dilemmas, contradictions, and challenges of Latin American education. I will end by saying that I believe that, for those who were able to know Paulo Freire and who have a vocation for research, as I think I do, it was natural to want to be as close to him as possible in order to better understand his thoughts. Although Paulo was not shy, he was very private and not every-body knew what was on his mind, despite his great communicative skills and public voluptuousness. It seems important to me—in addition to the philosophical and biographical studies we have been conducting all these years—to try to focus on his last years and on the political impact of his work, especially his decision-making process. For that reason I worked very intensely with him when I was his adviser in São Paulo, at the time he was Secretary of Education (1989–1991). The end result of that experience was a book written with two colleagues of mine, Pilar O'Cadiz and Pia Wong, who were writing their individual doctoral dissertations on Freire's tenure in the Secretariat. Pilar wrote her dissertation with me at UCLA, and Pia Wong wrote hers under Martin Carnoy at Stanford. Later on, the three of us put our notes together and wrote a book published in English as *Democracy and Education: Paulo Freire, Social Movements and Educational Reform in São Paulo* that, without any doubt, is one of the few empirical investigations of the experience. This book has not yet been translated into Spanish, although it is being translated into Portuguese in Lisbon.

AA: Moving to a more specific level of your academic work, Carlos, how do you deal with the theoretical and methodological problems of the investigations you conduct?

CAT: Each investigation presents different challenges, but there is no doubt the kind of work I do has a strong theoretical bias. So I like to think about the problems I am analyzing, beginning with their theoretical implications. There is undoubtedly a strong personal inclination toward the political analysis of education in my work which is partly due to the socialization that I received during my stay in Mexico, my education in Argentina and on my numerous visits to Latin America. One cannot think of education without thinking of politics. So I would say that I usually start with a theoretical framework, which is always a combination of sociology and the political economy of education with a strong emphasis on the theory of the state that helps me define certain directions in order to think about the problem at hand. Although I have enormous respect for positivist methodologies, especially the more quantitative aspects of certain logics and research techniques, I prefer to use qualitative analyses with a strong historical, even ethnographic, emphasis to be able to account for the problems we face. It is very difficult to respond in the abstract to a question like this one, because each investigation presents its own peculiarities. For example, I conducted a multinational investigation in which I collaborated with very distinguished Latin American researchers, among them Carlos Muñoz Izquierdo and Silvia Schmelkes in Mexico. It was a comparison of adult education in Tanzania, Canada and Mexico, and that necessitated a series of discussions. We had Pablo Latapí as an advisor and other people of great worth. It was necessary to make many decisions—what language should be used for the interviews, etc.—and many of them had to do with the selection of a sample that would be interesting from an analytical point of view without necessarily having to be representative, given the substantial differences between the three countries. There were also methodological complications when it came to techniques of data collection and that was a great challenge. It was already a challenge to coordinate a group of such talented people, coming from different traditions, with different languages and research experience. And it was extremely challenging to generate a research model that took into account the wealth of ideas and information that such an interesting group would produce. As difficult as it is to do comparative research, it is even more difficult if the research is conducted in different languages with different cultures, attempting to understand aspects that are closely tied to the popular culture of each country.

Now I am finishing my second major project—an investigation of six countries—and it is even more complex than the previous one, because here not only do we have different languages and different cultures, but also tremendously different cultural traditions. Here we have the encounter of the East and the West; we have the presence of Asia and the presence of two of the world's most developed nations, the United States and Japan. There is also Canada, a country that is among the seven most powerful on the planet. And then, of course, countries that have an enormous weight in the worldwide economy, like Korea and Mexico, and a country that has a little less weight and that is not at the same economic level, Argentina. This implies that the historical dynamics, the type of political discussion by country, the type of state, even the educational models that we are analyzing, are all really different. But as we are focusing on the practices and policies that drive teachers' unions, it is from that nerve center that we explore the image that in all these countries—and in other countries of the world—has led to the establishment of certain neoliberal policies. This gives us a common nucleus, a lowest common denominator that allows us to make a comparison that I feel—as I said before—it will be extraordinarily difficult to establish. It is very difficult to answer your question, since I would say, from a phenomenological viewpoint, each research project has its own demons, its own ghosts, and its own possibilities of resolution.

AA: Carlos, although you keep in frequent contact with colleagues from Mexico and the rest of Latin America, you are an academic that studies education from the United States. What advantages and disadvantages do you feel this gives you?

CAT: That is a very interesting question that would perhaps demand a more detailed discussion. I will try to be brief in my response. There is no doubt that my training, the fact that I speak English with an accent, the kind of analysis that I do, my theoretical models (which come from German critical social theory advanced by the so-called "Frankfurt School," which is not prevalent in the United States) make me an academic who does not clearly reflect the general practices of the American academy. This has its advantages and disadvantages. On the one hand, I have a very simple advantage that seems like a joke: since English is my second language, my colleagues are much more tolerant of me than of each other so that, in faculty and committee meetings, I can speak at greater length than they allow themselves, due to the unwritten rules about speaking clearly, concisely, and briefly. When one goes to a French restaurant and the chef appears, speaking English with a French accent, one may feel that the food is richer—there is some sort of legitimizing process, which grants additional authenticity to the product. When I teach a course in Latin American education, my accent makes conversation with the students take on a whole new light and weight. It is a kind of joke, but I believe that one has to take what can be seen as a weakness—the fact that I learned English when I was thirty years old and beginning my doctorate at Stanford and have a pronounced accent—and transform it into a strength.

Another aspect to take into account is the international part. I am an academic who is working on international issues, which makes me part of a distinct minority at a university like UCLA. There is no doubt that many of my international interests, such as education in Latin America and my studies of the Pacific Rim, are of little concern to my colleagues, who are more worried about racial problems in the schools of Los Angeles or how teaching elementary school mathematics can be improved. Therefore, in the end, one becomes a kind of prophet in the desert. Nevertheless, since the notion of diversity is celebrated in the American academy, it is important to have people like me around to remind them that a world exists outside UCLA and Los Angeles, that there is a very strong tension between education and politics, that there are certain categorical imperatives such as social justice, individual responsibility, and what in English is called caring, i.e., the capacity to give and to love. There is no reason why these imperatives should be subsumed and vanish in an age of technological reproduction and positivist logic.

I would say that my academic life in the United States has been very satisfactory; I cannot complain. I feel very comfortable at UCLA: I am director of a Latin American Center and, as a professor from a professional school, this is quite unusual given the predominance of professors from social science departments like history, political science, and sociology, which have traditionally held hegemony in Latin American studies in the United States. I have had a great deal of support here and, certainly, we Latin Americans work very hard and totally commit ourselves to the kinds of research we do.

I would add another element, perhaps a very personal one, but I think it is essential to take one's own situation into account when planning a career. I am an immigrant, so I have certain advantages and disadvantages. The University is a "very demanding lover," especially for an immigrant. Immigrants customarily lack certain affective relationships, with the exception of their immediate families, since it is not easy to work full time and make new friendships in one's adopted country. So much of my work is concentrated around the University, which is why I define it in the words of my dear friend, Dr. Humberto Muñoz, as a "very demanding lover." The truth is, I have worked very intensely and I believe that is reflected in my productivity and in the respect I get in the professional associations in which I participate. But I also believe that there are very limiting aspects to being an immigrant. There is a certain sense of the provisional in what one does and what one is; on the other hand, paradoxically, although I struggle in the space provided, I am not party to the real story, the specific political struggles at the core of US party politics. Although I want to contribute to the debates within this country, I never know if eventually I will return to Argentina or to Mexico, or continue to live as a political intellectual in two or three different conceptual, political, and historical spaces. Finally, the fact that I am an observer of Latin American politics causes my attention to be more focused on the Latin American part of the continent than on the American part, which also has its advantages and disadvantages.

AA: Carlos, thank you for your time and your very interesting ideas. A final question: what would you advise young students, and not so young ones, who are starting careers in the analysis of the educational problems of Mexico and Latin America?

CAT: I would say the following: first, do not enter this profession if you want an easy life. The analysis of the educational and sociopolitical problems of education generates a series of very intimate personal contradictions that need to be recognized, accepted and, if possible, overcome. This profession lacks the glamour of other professions and does not have the economic compensation or the social visibility of some occupations. So I would say that it is important to have a real vocation to be an educational researcher. This seems to be a fundamental question in the practice of educational research. Second, I would say that one has to recognize that there is an intimate relationship between education and politics. It is not possible to enter into this profession and maintain a strictly objective vision of reality, as if reality were something outside oneself to be studied, manipulated, and understood. We cannot be neutral when confronting the phenomena we study and the kinds of demands they present. We investigate reality as active participants in the process, attempting to transform it in explicit directions according to certain values that we accept and assume. This is a discipline of disciplines. In a way, education synthesizes many of the developments in the social sciences. This discipline of disciplines, or multidiscipline, requires immense rigor and very serious work. In Latin America, I am afraid that we have abused the educational essay, although it may be the best that has been seen. I think we need to train people to combine the political, literary, or educative essay with rigorous empirical investigation. Those academics who can walk both paths are going to provide a great contribution to pedagogy, to education in general and, of course, to the great investigators of Latin America. I will mention a peerless example, Dr. Pablo Latapí, who has great literary knowledge, is an extraordinary writer and a rigorous researcher of educational problems, producing what might be called "scientific journalism." It is necessary to learn from the performance of those who have been pioneers in their specific fields, because the avenues they have opened and their principles are, generally, what allows us to continue the search for wider vistas of coexistence and justice in democracies that are still maturing in a utopian sense.

Notes

NOTES TO THE INTRODUCTION

1. See Carlos Alberto Torres (editor), *La praxis educativa y la acción cultural liberadora de Paulo Freire*. Valencia, Spain: DENES-Instituto Paulo Freire, Edicions del CreC, 2005, p. 159.
2. See Paulo Freire, *Pedagogy of Freedom: Ethics, Democracy, and Civic Courage*. Lahman, New York1998.
3. See Carlos Alberto Torres (editor), *Op. cit.*, p. 160.
4. A book that has recently been reprinted, with new introductions, in celebration of the thirtieth anniversary of its publication by the Paulo Freire Institute of Spain. See Carlos Alberto Torres (editor), *Op. cit.*
5. Freire, in Torres, *Op. cit.*, p. 161.
6. Freire, in Torres, *Op. cit.*, p. 160.
7. The Paulo Freire Institute of São Paulo, from where I wrote some of the chapters of this book, has launched a project inspired by the work of Moacir Gadotti and José Eustáquio Romão to impel a model of planetary consciousness that would link education, ecology, and social rights with the struggles of the major social movements of the day, as evidenced in the World Social Forum and World Educational Forum. For an analysis of the premises of this new anti-globalization model, see the work of Boaventura de Sousa Santos (in Rhoads and Torres, 2006); Moacir Gadotti, "Pedagogia da terra: Ecopedagogia e educação sustentável." Paper presented at Conferência Continental das Américas, December 1998, in Cuiabá (MT), and during the Primeiro Encontro Internacional da Carta da Terra na Perspectiva da Educação, organized by the Instituto Paulo Freire, Conselho da Terra and UNESCO, São Paulo, Brazil, August 23–26, 1999. See also José Eustáquio Romão, "Pedagogia Sociológica ou Sociologia Pedagógica. Paulo Freire e a Sociologia da Educação." In Antonio Teodoro and Carlos Alberto Torres (organizadores), *Educação, Critica e Utopia. Perspectivas para o século XXI*. Porto, Afrontamento, 2005. (In English, Carlos Alberto Torres and Antonio Teodoro (editors), *Critique and Utopia. New Developments in the Sociology of Education in the Twenty-First Century*, Lahman MD: Rowman and Littlefield, 2007.
8. Freire, in Torres, *Op. cit.*, p. 164.

NOTES TO CHAPTER 1

1. Paper originally presented to the Meeting of the Fondazione Liberal, Milan, Italy, May 15–17, 2003.

2. Mark Twain, *Letters from the Earth*, cited in Carlos Alberto Torres, *Democracy, Education and Multiculturalism: Dilemmas of Citizenship in a Global World*. Lanham, MD: Rowman and Littlefield, 1998, p. 167.
3. David Held (editor), *Political Theory Today*. Stanford, CA: Stanford University Press, 1991, p. 9.
4. Robert B. Reich, *Education and the New Economy*, Washington, DC: National Education Association, 1988; Robert Reich, *The Works of Nations. Preparing Ourselves for 21st Century Capitalism*. New York: Vintage Books, 1992.
5. Kenichi Ohmae, *The Borderless World: Power and Strategy in the Interlinked World Economy*. New York: Harber Business, 1990; Kenichi Ohmae, *The End of the Nation-State: The Rise of Regional Economies*. New York: Free Press, 1995.
6. James O'Connor, *The Fiscal Crisis of the State*. New York: St. Martins Press, 1973.
7. Jürgen Habermas, *Legitimation Crisis*. Edited and translated by Jeremy J. Shapiro. Boston: Beacon, 1975.
8. Carlos Alberto Torres, *Op. cit.*, p. 14. From a postmodern perspective, Fredric Jameson defines the characteristics of postmodernism as the cultural logic of late capitalism. Fredric Jameson, *Postmodernism or the Cultural Logic of Late Capitalism*. Durham, NC: Duke University Press, 1991.
9. See António Teodoro, "Educational Policies and New Ways of Governance in a Transnationalization Period." In Carlos Alberto Torres and Ari Antikainen (editors), *The International Handbook on the Sociology of Education*. Lanham, MD: Rowman and Littlefield, 2003, p. 198.
10. Martin Carnoy, "El impacto de la mundialización en las estrategias de reforma educativa." *Revista de Educación*, número extraordinario, 2001, pp. 101–110; Martin Carnoy, "La articulación de las reformas educativas en la economía mundial." pp. 111–120.
11. Quoted in Robert A. Rhoads, Carlos A. Torres, and Andrea Brewster, "Turmoil and Transition in Latin American Higher Education: The Cases of Argentina and Mexico." Paper presented at the Center for the Studies in Higher Education at the University of California, Berkeley, May 5, 2003, p. 16.
12. http://www.civilrightsproject.harvard.edu/research/dropouts/dropouts05.php
13. This has been one of the key strategies currently implemented by the schools districts in the California as a way to cope with the state's growing deficit. The 2003 deficit was estimated to be 32 billion dollars that needed to be balanced in two years. This strategy sought to override the law that California classrooms should have no more than 20 students per teacher; therefore, in 2003, an increase in class size led to a massive layoff of the teachers without tenure and with less seniority.
14. Increasing class size as a way to cope with burgeoning enrollments result in increasing exploitation of teachers, with diminishing real salaries per capita. An analysis of a historical situation using Mexico as a case in point is found in Daniel A. Morales-Gómez and Carlos Alberto Torres, *The State, Corporatist Politics, and Educational Policy-Making in Mexico (1970–1988)*. New York: Praeger, 1990.
15. Carnoy, *Op. cit.*, p. 107. Author's translation.
16. Malkit Kaur, "Globalization and Women: Some Likely Consequences." In Raj Mohini Sethi (editor), *Globalization, Culture and Women's Development*. Jaipur, India: Rawat Publications, 1999, p. 126.
17. The Group of Seven, including Russia, is composed of eight countries.
18. One of the best known critics of the International Monetary Fund and the model of globalization sponsored by multilateral organizations is the Nobel Price-winning economist, George Stingler, who gave this fancy

title—*Globalization and Its Discontents*—to his best-selling book. There is no question in my mind of the influence of Freud's *Civilization and Its Discontents* in Stingler's title. Yet, there are a number of other voices that are critical of globalization. Influential French sociologist Pierre Bourdieu was an acerbic critic of neoliberal globalization. Referring to the events of Genoa, Italy, in which anti-globalization critics were confronted with severe force, he argued that "A violência de massas tem, ao menos, alguma utilidade: força os principais atores do neoliberalismo, que gostam de parecer calmos, serenos, e racionais, a mostrarem sua própria violência." Pierre Bourdieu, "O Neoliberalismo é como a sida." Interview by Romain Leick. *Diário de Notícias*, 21 July 2001, p. 18. Hence, the violence of the globalizers is equated to a devastating disease like AIDS.

19. Robert A. Rhoads, Carlos A. Torres, and Andrea Brewster, *Op. cit.*
20. Unlike the Portuguese colonization, the Spanish colonizers implanted institutions of higher education very early in the settlement process in the new 'discovered' lands. For instance, the Autonomous University of Santo Domingo was founded on October 28, 1538, less than fifty years after Columbus's voyage to America. The process continued, and many other universities were quickly established after settlement—for instance, the Autonomous University of Córdoba, in Argentina, was founded in 1613.
21. For an international analysis and critique of the entrepreneurial university model, see Jan Currie and Janice Newson (editors), *Universities and Globalization. Critical Perspectives*. Thousand Oaks, CA: Sage Publications, 1998. A defense of the triple helix model of university–industry–government relations, advocating that "Calculations of social profit has become as important as scientific profit" (p. 152) could be found in Henry Hetzkowitz and Loet Leydesdorff (editors), *Universities and the Global Knowledge Economy*. London: Pinter, 1997.
22. Robert A. Rhoads, Carlos A. Torres, and Andrea Brewster, *Op. cit.*, p. 12.
23. Robert A. Rhoads, Carlos A. Torres, and Andrea Brewster, *Op. cit.*, p. 28.
24. Robert A. Rhoads, Carlos A. Torres, and Andrea Brewster, *Op. cit.*, p. 12.
25. Robert A. Rhoads, Carlos A. Torres, and Andrea Brewster, *Op. cit.*, p. 29. For a more detailed analysis of the political economy of higher education in the Americas, see Robert A. Rhoads and Carlos A. Torres (editors), *The University, State, and Market. The Political Economy of Globalization in the Americas*. Stanford, CA: Stanford University Press, 2006.
26. Robert A. Rhoads, Carlos A. Torres, and Andrea Brewster, *Op. cit.*, p. 29.
27. Nuhoglu Soysal, *Limits of Citizenship: Migrants and Postnational Membership in Europe*. Chicago: University of Chicago Press, 1994, pp. 164–165.
28. Nuhoglu Soysal, *Op. cit.*, p. 166
29. Carlos Alberto Torres, *Op. cit.*, p. 85.
30. Charlote Bunch, "Women's Human Rights. The Challenges of Global Feminism and Diversity." In Marianne Dekoven, (editor), *Feminist Locations. Global and Local, Theory and Practice*. New Brunswick, NJ: Rutgers University Press, 2001, pp. 138–139.
31. Charlote Bunch, *Op. cit.*
32. This section benefits from my work in Carlos Alberto Torres, "Comparative Education: The Dialectics of Globalization and its Discontents." In Robert Arnove and Carlos Alberto Torres (editors), *Comparative Education: The Dialectics of the Global and the Local*, Third edition. Lanham, MD: Rowman and Littlefield, 2007
33. Michael Apple, "Patriotism, Pedagogy, and Freedom: On the Educational Meanings of September 11th." *The Teachers College Record*, 2002; 104 (8): pp. 1760–1772, quote on page 1770. This entire issue of *Teachers' College*

Record is devoted to the discussion of the events of September 11ᵗʰ and its impact on the life of the schools, teachers, and students. At a more theoretical level, many articles tackle the meaning of September 11ᵗʰ for the discussion of patriotism versus cosmopolitanism in the constitution of democratic life.

34. Ravinder Sidhu, "Selling Futures to Foreign Students: Global Education Markets." manuscript, University of Queensland, Australia, p. 12. International educational trade, however, is not going to be deeply affected because of its sheer magnitude: "By the first decade of the twenty-first century international trade in education services had become a dynamic global industry. While the full value of the industry on a worldwide scale is difficult to estimate with accuracy, trade at the higher education level was estimated at over US$27 billion per annum in the 1990's." Tim Mazzarol and Geoffrey Norman Soutar, *The Global Market for Higher Education. Sustainable Competitive Strategies for the New Millennium.* Cheltenham, United Kingdom, Edward Elgar 2001, p. 157. Another example is programs of Masters in Business Administration (MBA). The authors report that in 1996, there were 80,000 foreign joint ventures operating MBAs in China to train 250,000 managers (p. 159).

35. Michael Apple, *Op. cit.*, pp. 1770–1771.

36. Neena Vyas, "Modi for Reforming 'Madrassas.'" *The Hindu*, June 14, 2002.

37. Jerry Mander and Edward Goldsmith, *The Case Against the Global Economy and for a Turn Toward the Local.* San Francisco: Sierra Books, 1996; Nick Burbules and Carlos A. Torres (editors), *Globalization and Education: Critical Analysis.* New York: Routlege, 2000.

38. Robert Burbach, *Globalization and Postmodern Politics: From Zapatists to High-Tech Robber Barons.* London: Pluto Press, 2001; N. C. Burbules and C. A. Torres, "Globalization and Education: An Introduction," N. C. Burbules and C. A. Torres (editors), *Globalization and Education: Critical Perspectives.* New York: Routledge, 2000, pp. 1–26.; D. Kellner, "Globalization and New Social Movements: Lessons for Critical Theory and Pedagogy," N. C. Burbules and C. A. Torres *Op. cit.*, pp. 299–321; S. Slaughter and D. L. Leslie, *Academic Capitalism: Politics, Policies, and the Entrepreneurial University.* Baltimore, MD: Johns Hopkins University Press, 1997; R. Went, *Globalization: Neoliberal Challenge, Radical Responses.* London: Pluto Press, 2000; Robert A. Rhoads, "Globalization and Resistance in Mexico and the United States: The Global Potemkin Village." Paper submitted to Higher Education, UCLA, Los Angeles, CA; Various, *Alternatives to Economic Globalization. A Better World is Possible. A Report of the International Forum on Globalization.* San Francisco: Berrett-Koehler Publisher, 2002.

39. José Eustéquio Romão, *Globalización o Planetarización. Las Trampas del Discurso Hegemónico.* São Paulo: Instituto Paulo Freire, 2001; Octavio Ianni, *A era do Globalismo.* Rio de Janeiro: Civilização Brasileira, 1996; Octavio Ianni. *A Sociedade Global.* Rio de Janeiro: Civilização Brasileira, 1993.

40. Cynthia Saltzman, "The Many Faces of Activism." In Marianne Dekoven (editor). *Op. cit.*, p. 194.

41. See http://www.amnestyusa.org/war-on-terror/unilateralism.html.

42. Paulo Freire. *Pedagogy of the City.* Cited in Carlos Alberto Torres, *Democracy, Education and Multiculturalism. Op. cit.*, p. 161.

NOTES TO CHAPTER 2

1. Paper prepared for the meeting "Extending the Boundaries of Democracy: Two Decades of Education Reform and Inclusion Policies." Bellagio, Italy, December 9–13, 2002.

2. Expert knowledge refers to both a multidimentional prototype, as described by the author of the triarchic theory of intelligence, R. J. Sternberg, in his work—e.g., that expertise is domain-specific—and the organization of the acquisition of expertise, usually linking expert knowledge and specific organizations or institutions of knowledge production, distribution, and consumption. See the following works: R.J. Sternberg, *Intelligence, Information Processing, and Analogical Reasoning*. Hillsdale, NJ: Erlbaum, 1977; R.J. Sternberg, *Beyond IQ*. New York: Cambridge University Press, 1985; R.J. Sternberg, "Criteria for Intellectual Skills Training." *Educational Researcher*, 1983; 12: 6–12; R.J. Sternberg, "Cognitive Conceptions of Expertise." In P. J. Feltovich, K. M. Ford, annd R.R. Hoffman (editors), *Expertise in Context: Human and Machine*. Menlo Park, CA: AAAI Press/The MIT Press, 1997, pp. 149–162; Päivi Tynjälä, "Towards Expert Knowledge? A Comparison Between a Constructivist and a Traditional Learning Environment in the University." *International Journal of Educational Research*, 1999; 31: 355–442.

3. Päivi Tynjälä, *Op. cit.*, p. 359.

4. See Doug Bandow and Ian Vásquez (editors), *Perpetuating Poverty: The World Bank, the IMF, and the Developing World*. Washington, D. C.: CATO Institute, 1994.

5. See John Harriss, *Depoliticizing Development: The World Bank and Social Capital*. London: Anthem Press-Wimbledon Publishing2002, p. 25.

6. *Ibid.*, p. 97.

7. Given the importance of James Coleman's pioneering work on social capital, I choose this quotation to illustrate some of the premises behind the theoretical work of the World Bank. See James Coleman, *Foundations of Social Theory*. Cambridge, MA: Harvard University Press, 1990, p. 27.

8. See Larissa Lomnitz and Ana Melnick, *Chile's Middle Class: A Struggle for Survival in the Face of Neoliberalism*. Boulder, CO: Lynne Rienner Publishers, 1991.

9. Quoted in Joel Samoff, "More, Less, None? Human Resource Development: Responses to Economic Constraint." Palo Alto, CA: June 1990, mimeograph, p. 21; Fernando Reimers, "Educación para todos en América Latina en el Siglo XXI. Los desafios de la estabilización, el ajuste y los mandatos de Jomtien." Paper presented to the workshop on Poverty, Adjustment, and Infant Survival, organized by UNESCO, Lima, Peru, December 3–6, 1990, p. 16.

10. There are several premises of my analysis that need to be clarified at the outset. First, while I focus on the World Bank's practices of expert knowledge and policies of external aid, the aim of my analysis is more general, analyzing the perils of external aid and expertise of regulatory institutions of capitalism. Second, there is no question in my mind that the logic of institutional activism in no way morally excuses individual actions. Yet, individual actions may not be entirely blamed for their biased premises, and worse yet, for biased results. Third, regulatory institutions of capitalism refer to the notion advanced by the Neo-Marxist French regulation school identifying the development of Fordism as a monopolistic model of development, replacing the previous competitive model of development, changes that are well described and analyzed by P. Baran and P. Sweezy in their classic book *Monopoly Capital* (New York: Monthly Review Press, 1966). There are domestic institutions of capitalist regulation (mostly to regulate wage prices) and international institutions of capitalist regulation (mostly to regulate monetary systems and methods of payments, international trade regulations, and economic and military treaties) that facilitate a worldwide regime of accumulation and mode of regulation. Financial institutions resulting from the Bretton Woods agreement at the end

of World War II are characteristically regulatory institutions, replacing the gold standard with credit money tied to the US dollar, the currency of the dominant world economy, which may be soon replaced by the Euro as the international monetary benchmark. For a consistent economic history and theory of these changes in modes of accumulation and regulation, from pre-Fordism to Fordism and Post-Fordism, see D. J. Frantzen, *Growth and Crisis in Post-War Capitalism*. Aldershot, UK: Darmouth Publishing, and Gower Publishing, 1990, pp. 58–138.

11. Debates about the definition of globalization are as ubiquitous as the term itself. For the sake of clarity in this chapter, the term *globalization* refers to "a range of trends towards increasing interconnection in a number of different dimensions—including financial, production, and labor markets, telecommunications, information, and transportation networks, security systems, and culture and lifestyles—that result in unforeseen causal interdependencies between actions and events in distant parts of the globe." Ciaran Cronin and Pablo de Greiff, "Introduction: Normative Responses to Current Challenges of Global Governance." In Ciaran Cronin and Pablo de Greiff, (editors), *Global Justice and Transnational Politics: Essays on the Moral and Political Challenges of Globalization*. Cambridge, MA: The MIT Press, 2002, p, 29, fn 1. For an extensive discussion about globalization in education, see my work with Nick Burbules (editors), *Globalization and Education: Critical Concepts*. New York: Routledge, 2000.

12. See the following works: Carlos Alberto Torres, "Editorial. Comparative Education: Requiem for Liberalism?" *Comparative Education Review*, November 2002; Raymond A. Morrow and Carlos Alberto Torres, *Social Theory and Education: A Critique of Theories of Social and Cultural Reproduction*. New York: SUNY Press, 1995; Carlos Alberto Torres; "La Educación del Futuro y los Dilemas de Nuestra Hora." *Cuadernos de Educación*, September 2002; Carlos Alberto Torres, "The State, Privatization and Educational Policy: A Critique of Neoliberalism in Latin America and Some Ethical and Political Implications." *Comparative Education*, 2002; 38(4) .

13. James Bovard, "The World Bank and the Impoverishment of Nations." In Doug Bandow and Ian Vásquez (editors), *Op. cit.*, p. 59.

14. For conservatives and liberals alike, the period of Robert McNamara as bank president (1968–1981) is the subject of heated controversy. A topic of criticism is the World Bank's lending policies, and particularly the ability of the World Bank to deal with the question of poverty in the Third World. For a conservative critique, see for instance, James Bovard, *Op. cit.*, pp. 59–74. For a liberal critique and defense of the World Bank, see Robert L. Ayres, *Banking on the Poor: The World Bank and World Poverty*. Cambridge, MA: The MIT Press, 1983. The recent controversy about World Bank President Paul Wolfowitz's peculiar understanding of ethics—he offered a pay raise to his girlfriend without consulting the Ethics Committee of the World Bank—places the Bank again in the eye of the storm of public opinion.

15. The Washington Consensus is composed of a group of financial institutions such as the IMF, the World Bank, the Inter-American Development Bank, the Export-Import Bank, among others, all located in Washington, D.C. (sometimes within blocks of each other, such as the World Bank and the Inter-American Development Bank), and all following—with few technical divergences—the same logic and neoliberal economic policies, which are part of the model of structural adjustment and stabilization. See Atilio Alberto Boron, *Estado, Capitalismo y Democracia en América Latina*. Buenos Aires: Ediciones Amago Mundi, 1991; Luis Carlos Bresser Pereira, "La

crisis de América Latin ¿Consenso de Washington o crisis fiscal?" *Pensamiento Iberoamericano*, 1991; 19; José Maria Fanelli, Roberto Frenkel, and Guillermo Rozenwurcel, "Growth and Structural Reform in Latin America: Where we Stand." Buenos Aires: documento CEDES 67, 1990.

16. They are distinct from the radical, pragmatic, neostructural school of the Economic Commision for Latin America (ECLA), or the adjustment with a human face promoted by UNICEF and the Society for International Development. Economic conditionality is required by the World Bank, the IMF, and the majority of institutions identified as the Washington Consensus.

17. Ian Culpitt, *Welfare and Citizenship: Beyond the Crisis of the Welfare State?* London: Sage Publications, 1992, p. 94.

18. Michael Moran and Maurice Wright, *The Market and the State: Studies in Interdependence*. New York: St. Martin's Press, 1991.

19. Interestingly enough, George Soros, recognized as a brilliant financier, is highly critical of what he considers 'market fundamentalism' in the capitalist global system. He argues that " . . . the prevailing view based on economic theory is that financial markets tend towards equilibrium. I contend that this is actually a false view of financial markets . . . this is not appropriate because financial markets basically discount the future. However, the future that they discount is not something independent of their own discounting mechanism." See George Soros, et al., "Against Market Fundamentalism: 'The Capitalist Threat' Reconsidered." In László Zsolnai, in cooperation with Wojciech W. Gasparski (editors), *Ethics and the Future of Capitalism*. Piscataway, NJ: Transaction Publishers, 2002, pp. 24–25; 26.

20. Ravi Ramamurti, "Privatization and the Latin American Debt Problem." In Robert Grosse (editor), *Private Sector Solutions to the Latin American Debt Problem*. Piscataway, NJ: Transaction Publishers, North-South Center and the University of Miami, 1991, p. 153.

21. *Op. cit.*, p. 168.

22. *Op. cit.*, p. 169.

23. Daniel Morales-Gómez and Carlos Alberto Torres, "Education for All: Prospects and Implications for Latin America in the 1990s." In Carlos Alberto Torres (editor), *Education and Social Change in Latin America*. Melbourne, Australia: James Nicholas Publisher, 1994.

24. José Luis Coraggio, "Human Capital: the World Bank's Approach to Education in Latin America." in J. Cavanagh, D. Wysham, and M. Arruda (editors), *Beyond Bretton Woods: Alternatives to the Global Economic Order*. London: Institute for Policy Studies and Transnational Institute and Pluto Press, 1994, p. 168.

25. See Carlos Alberto Torres, "A Critical Review of Education for All (EFA) Background Documents," *Perspectives on Education for All*. Ottawa, Canada: IDRC-MR295e, April 1991, pp. 1–20; Daniel Morales-Gómez and Carlos Alberto Torres, *Op. cit.* . A similar analysis is found in Fernando Reimers, "Education for All in Latin America in the XXI Century and the Challenges of External Indebtedness." In Carlos Alberto Torres, *Op. cit.*, p..

26. Michael Bujazan, Sharon E. Hare, Thomas J. La Belle, and Lisa Stafford, "International Agency Assistance to Education in Latin America and the Caribbean, 1970–1984: Technical and Political Decision-Making." *Comparative Education*, 1987; 23(3): 161–170.

27. The World Bank was the main participant in the conference on Education for All, held in March 1990 in Jomtien, Thailand, and co-sponsored by UNICEF, UNESCO, and UNDP.

28. Bruce Fuller, *Raising School Quality in Developing Countries: What Investments Boost Learning.* Washington, D.C.: The World Bank, 1986, p. 21.
29. Joel Samoff, "From Lighting a Torch on Kilimanjaro to Surviving in a Shantytown: Education and Financial Crisis in Tanzania." Case study presented to the UNESCO-International Labor Organization Commission on Austerity, Adjustment and Human Resources, 1992.
30. I have heard too many times, from functionaries of these international organizations attempting to shelter themselves from criticism for their actions and high salaries, that if they don't get their paycheck, someone else will.
31. David Plank, "Three Reports from the World Bank." Manuscript, Pittsburgh, PA, 1991.
32. See, for example, Joel Samoff, "Chaos and Uncertainty in Development." Paper prepared for the XV World Congress of the International Political Science Association, Buenos Aires, Argentina, July 21–25, 1991; Joel Samoff, "Triumphalism, Tarzan and Other Influences: Teaching About Africa in the 1990s." Manuscript, Palo Alto, CA, 1993. There are many examples of informed criticisms of the positivistic model of educational planning. See Rolland Paulston, "Mapping Paradigms and Theories in Comparative Education." Paper presented to the Comparative and International Education Society Annual Meeting, Annapolis, MD, March 1992; Hans N. Weiler, "Why Reforms Fail: The Politics of Education in France and the Federal Republic of Germany." *Journal of Curriculum Studies,* 1989; 21: 291–305. For a postmodern analysis with educational references, see Henry Giroux and Peter McLaren, "America 2000 and the Politics of Erasure: Democracy and Cultural Difference Under Siege." *International Journal of Educational Reform,* 1992; 1(2): 99–100.
33. Nancy C. M. Hartsock, "The Feminist Standpoint: Developing the Grounds for a Specifically Feminist Historical Materialism." In Sandra Harding (editor), *Feminism and Methodology.* Bloomington, IN: University of Indiana Press, 1987, p. 162.
34. For a description and analysis of the overall policy experience, see Carlos Alberto Torres, "Paulo Freire as Secretary of Education in the Municipality of São Paulo." *Comparative Education Review,* 1994; 382: 181–214. See also Pilar O'Cadiz, Pia Linquist Wong, and Carlos Alberto Torres, *Education and Democracy: Paulo Freire, Social Movements, and Educational Reform in São Paulo.* Bolder, CO: Westview Press, 1998.
35. Joseph Rouse, *Knowledge and Power: Toward a Political Philosophy of Science.* Ithaca, NY: Cornell University Press, 1987, p. 244.

NOTES TO CHAPTER 3

1. Published in a Symposium on Education in a special issue of *New Politics: A Journal of Socialist Thought,* coordinated by Lois Weiner, 2005.
2. Conferación de trabajadores de la Educación de la República Argentina. (Educational Worker's Confederation of the Argentine Republic).
3. Levin and Belfield, 2004: 1.
4. De Bray, 2003: 57.
5. De Bray, 2003: 62.
6. Saravia & Miranda, 2004: 608.
7. *Ibid.*
8. De Bray, 2003: 63.
9. E. San Juan Jr., 2002.
10. Rhoads and Torres, 2006. *Op. cit.*

11. Linda Bell, 2003
12. htpp://www.rethinkingschools.org/special_reports/bushplan/hoax.html.
13. Carlos Ovando, 2004.
14. Fox and Brown, 2000: 12.
15. McCarthy, 1998; Jacoby, 1994; Torres, 1998.
16. Dimitriadis and Carlson, 2003.

NOTES TO CHAPTER 4

1. Written after a conversation with Antonio Teodoro, former general secretary and President of the Portuguese Teacher Unions, and currently professor at the Universidade Lusófona de Humanidades e Tecnologías, in Lisbon, Portugal. The conversation took place March 22, 2000 in Lisbon.
2. Conferación de trabajadores de la Educación de la República Argentina. (Educational Worker's Confederation of the Argentine Republic).
3. Burbules and Torres (editors), *Globalization and Education: Critical Concepts*. New York: Routledge, 2000.
4. *Ibid.*, p. 15.
5. *Ibid.*, p. 15.
6. This could be expressed in the monopoly of education as supplier of education, as the fact that the whole market operates under the same conditions, the same legislation, standardized curriculum, as such and systems of accreditation all combine to govern the state educational regime.
7. The first of April 1997, CTERA set up a white tent in from of the Argentine Congress to challenge several policies of the neoliberal government of President Carlos Saúl Menem. They requested a new law of educational financing and the derogation of the Federal Law of Education. The protest lasted for 1,003 days. With a total of 1,380 teachers fasting in this period, more than 2.8 million people visited the White Tent, included representatives of 7,000 schools in the nation. The White Tent became a symbol of anti-neoliberal policies, and has been credited to be one of the key experiences that undermined Menem's reelection.
8. This analysis emerges from several documents produced in the context of the research project on teachers unions and the state with a policy comparison of Japan, Korea, Mexico, Argentina, Canada, and the United States, coordinated by Carlos Alberto Torres, with the collaboration of Julie Thompson (USA), Seewha Cho (USA/Korea), Jerry Kachur (Canada), Aurora Loyo (Mexico), Marcela Mollis (Argentina), and Akio Nagao (Japan) as principal investigators.
9. See Peter, Marshall, and Fitzimons in Burbules and Torres, *Op. cit.*, p. 127.
10. *Ibid.*
11. *Ibid.*

NOTES TO CHAPTER 5

1. Carlos Alberto Torres. *The Political Pedagogy of Paulo Freire*, Introduction. In Paulo Freire, *Politics and Education*. Los Angeles: Latin American Center, 1998.
2. For more information about the Paulo Freire Institute in São Paulo, see our home page at http//ppbr.com/ipf.
3. Paulo Freire, *Pedagogy of the Oppressed*. Montevideo, Uruguay: Editorial Tierra Nueva, 1972, p. 19.
4. Freire, in this book, p. 56.

5. Freire, in this book, p. 24.
6. Freire, in this book, p. 47.
7. Carlos Alberto Torres, *Leitura crítica de Paulo Freire, Op. cit.* can be consulted to elaborate the preceding analysis. See also the introductory chapter of Carlos Alberto Torres, *Paulo Freire: Educación y Concientización.* Salamanca: Ediciones Sigueme, 1980.
8. Freire, in this book, p. 93.
9. Freire, in this book, p. 66.
10. There are many exemplary books analyzing the lifework of Paulo Freire and the implications of his *Pedagogy of the Oppressed* for contemporary education, too numerous to be listed here. Yet, to give the reader a bit of the flavor of the discussions, the gist of the arguments, and the possibilities of the analysis, see for instance, Carlos Alberto Torres (editor), *Leitura crítica de Paulo Freire.* São Paulo: Loyola, 1978; Carlos Alberto Torres, *Paulo Freire: Educación y Concientización.* Salamanca: Ediciones Sigueme, 1980; Frank Youngman, *Adult Education and Socialist Pedagogy,* London: Croom Helm, 1986; Henry A. Giroux, "Introduction."In *Paulo Freire, The Politics of Education. Culture, Power and Liberation.* South Hadley, MA: Bergin & Garvey Publishers, 1985, pp. xi–xxv; Peter McLaren and Peter Leonard (editors), *Paulo Freire. A Critical Encounter.* New York: Routledge, 1993; Moacir Gadotti, *Reading Paulo Freire. His Life and Work.* Albany, NY: State University of New York Press, 1994; Carlos Alberto Torres, *Estudios Freireanos.* Buenos Aires: Libros del Quirquincho, 1995.
11. Freire, in this book, p. 46.
12. See Carlos Alberto Torres (editor), *Leitura crítica de Paulo Freire.* São Paulo: Loyola, 1978.
13. Freire, in this book, p. 31.
14. See, on this subject, Fausto Franco, *El hombre; construción progresiva,* Madrid, 1973, pp. 9–83 and 208–22. See also K. C. Abraham, "Education for Revolution: The Significance of Paulo Freire's Thought." *Religion and Society* (Bengala) 1973; 20: 29–37.
15. See J. Arroyo, *Paulo Freire: su ideología y su método,* Zaragoza, n.d.; and, above all, J. Ruiz Olabuenaga, P. Morales, M. Marragun, *Paulo Freire: concientización y andragogía.* Buenos Aires, 1975, p. 257.
16. See for instance, Ira Shor and Paulo Freire, *A Pedagogy for Liberation. Dialogues on Transforming Education.* South Hadley, MA: Bergin & Garvey Publishers, 1987; Paulo Freire and Donaldo Macedo, *Literacy. Reading the Word and the World.* South Hadley, MA: Bergin & Garvey Publishers, 1987; Paulo Freire, with Moacir Gadotti, Ana María Saúl, and Carlos Alberto Torres, *L' Education dans la ville.* Paris: Païdeia, 1991.
17. Very often Paulo Freire is accused of being an eclectic lacking in originality. To refute the first part of that accusation (eclecticism), see Carlos Alberto Torres, "La dialéctica hegeliana y el pensamento lógico-estructural de Paulo Freire." *SIC* 1976; 383: 116–122. To consider the question of Freire's theoretical originality, the following text by Freire himself, in which he quotes John Dewey, can be instructive: "Originality is not in the fantastic but in the new use of known things." *Educación como práctica de la libertad,* Montevideo, Uruguay: Ediciones Tierra Nueva, 1971, p. 149.
18. Known as one of the most prominent political scientist in Brazil, Francisco C. Weffort has known the Freire family since their days of exile in Santiago de Chile in the mid-60s. In Santiago de Chile, Francisco C. Weffort met Magdalena Freire, the oldest of Freire's children, and married her. Weffort joined the PT (or Workers Party), the same political party that he founded together with a number of other Brazilian intellectuals and workers, including Paulo

Freire and Moacir Gadotti, in 1978. For a decade, Weffort was associated with the PT in a number of roles but later withdrew from the party. He was the Minister of Culture of Brazil under the leadership of Fernando Henrique Cardoso, President of Brazil, who is the former President of the International Sociological Association, and a noted Latin American sociologist who is considered one of the fathers of the theory of dependency, challenging capitalist models of development, but his administration followed a neoliberal political model in Brazil sponsored by a social–democratic government coalition.

19. See Francisco C. Weffort, "Educacão e política. Reflexões sociológicas sobre una pedagogía da liberdade," Introduction to *Paulo Freire: Educação como práctica de liberdade*. Rio de Janeiro: Paz e Terra, 1967, p. 7.

20. Freire, in this book, p. 38.

21. A few numbers can be faithful expressions of the magnitude of the problem: the northeast of Brazil in which Freire developed his initial pedagogical experiment in 1962 had some 15 million illiterates out of a population of 25 million inhabitants. Given that the task of increasing literacy implied, the increase of the population of electors (which provoked a notable rise in political support of the populist regime), the immediate political implications on this level of the process of literacy acquisition can be easily appreciated. For instance, in 1964, the year of the Brazilian *coup d' etat*, literacy training would have incorporated 80,000 new electors to the 90,000 already existing in the state of Sergipe alone. In Pernambuco, the mass of electors would have grown from 800,000 to 1,300,000. For a discussion of the political implications of the early Freire experiences with literacy training in Brazil, see the above-mentioned essay by Francisco C. Weffort, and also Thomas G. Sanders' essay, "The Paulo Freire Method: Literacy training and conscientization," American Universities Field Staff, *Report West Coast South America* 1968; 15: 18. For a broader theoretical perspective, see Carlos Alberto Torres, *The Politics of Nonformal Education in Latin America*. New York: Praeger, 1990.

22. See Pilar O'Cadiz, Carlos Alberto Torres, and Pia Wong, *Education and Democracy: Paulo Freire, Social Movements and Educational Reform in São Paulo, Brazil*. Bolder, CO: Westview Press.

23. See Francisco C. Weffort, *Op.cit.*, pp. 8–9.

24. *Conscientization* has been defined by Freire as follows: "The French 'prise de conscience,' to take consciousness of, is a normal way of being a human being. Conscientization is something which goes beyond the 'prise de conscience.' It is something which is starting from the ability of getting, of taking the 'prise de conscience.' Something which implies to analyze. It is a kind of reading the world rigorously or almost rigorously. It is the way of reading how society works. It is the way to understand better the problem of interests, the question of power. How to get power, what it means not to have power. Finally, conscientizing implies a deeper reading of reality, [and] the common sense goes beyond the common sense." Conversation with Carlos Alberto Torres, in "Learning to Read the World," videotape, ACCESS Network, Edmonton, Alberta, Canada, October 1990.

25. See Carlos Alberto Torres, "Education and the Archeology of Consciousness: Freire and Hegel." *Educational Theory*, 1994; 44 (4): 429–445.

26. Freire, in this book, p. 74.

27. Carlos Alberto Torres, *Education, Democracy and Multiculturalism. Dilemmas of Citizenship in a Global World*. Lahman, MD: Rowman and Littlefield, 1998a.

28. Amy Gutman, *Democratic Education*. Princeton, NJ: Princeton University Press, 1987.

29. Will Kymlicka and Wayne Norman, "Return of the Citizen: A Survey of Recent Work on Citizenship Theory." *Ethics* 1994;104: 368.
30. Freire, in this book, pp. 56–57.
31. See P. Freire, "La misión educativa de las iglesias en América Latina," *Contacto*, Mexico, 1972; 9(5): 32.
32. See Francisco C. Weffort, *Op. cit.*, p. 13.
33. Weffort asserts, confirming our line of argument, that, "this educator (Freire) knows that his task contains political implications and he knows, moreover, that these implications are in the interest of the common man and not of the elite. But he knows also that his field is pedagogy and not politics and that he cannot, as an educator, substitute the revolutionary politician interested in knowledge and structural transformation. He rejects the traditional notion of education as 'lever for progress,' would it make sense to oppose to this the equally ingenuous thesis of 'education as a lever for revolution'? A pedagogy of freedom can help popular politics since conscientization means an opening up to the comprehension of social structures as means of domination and violence. But the task of orienting this growth of awareness in a specifically political direction falls on the politician, not the educator." (Francisco C. Weffort, *Op. cit.*, p. 16).
34. See P. Freire, "Education, Liberation and the Church," *Study Encounter* 1973; 9(1).
35. Freire, in this book, page 85.
36. It is fitting to cite as sources the interviews that Paulo Freire did with different periodicals in our reflection on Freire. Among the most significant of his early period consult "Educación para un despertar de conciencia. Una charla con Paulo Freire." In Carlos Alberto Torres *Entreistas de Paulo Freire*, Mexico, Gerika, 1978. *Risk* 1970; 6 (1): 7–19; "Entrevista con Paulo Freire." *Cuadernos de educación* 1972; 26 ; and finally "Una conversación con Paulo Freire." *IDAC*, Document 1, Geneve, 1973, entitled *Conscientisation et introduction a la discussion avec Paulo Freire*. The brief but substantial conference held at the university of Buenos Aires in 1973 called "Seminario sobre la filosofía de la educación liberadora y sus aportes para la formulación de una pedagogía universitaria," organized by the Ministry of Culture and Education, held from 7–9 November 1973, was very enlightening for us. Freire's intervention can be appreciated under the title of *Conclusiones del seminario coordinado por Paulo Freire*, 25–29; the publication was printed as *Cuadernos de Pedagogía* 1974; 1. Two texts which deal with similar problems can be consulted: *Le processus d'alphabetisation politque*: Lutherische Monatshefte, 1970, which appeared under the title of "The Political Literacy Process: An Introduction," published in *IDOC Internacional* 1970; 40: 47–60, and also see "Literacy and the Possible Dream." *Prospects* 1976; 6(1):68–71. One of his last interviews appears in Carlos Alberto Torres, *Education, Power and Personal Biography*. New York: Routledge.
37. See F. Franco, *Op.cit.*, p. 89.
38. See P. Freire, *Educación como práctica de la libertad*, p. 145.
39. See P. Freire, *La misión educativa de las iglesias . . .* , pp. 17–18.
40. See P. Freire, *Pedagogía del oprimido*, Mexico, Siglo *xxi*, 1978, p. 189.

NOTES TO CHAPTER 6

1. See, for example Chapter 2 in this book. Also see Joel Samoff, "Chaos and Uncertainty in Development." Paper prepared for the XV World Congress of the International Political Science Association, Buenos Aires, Argentina,

July 21–25, 1991; "Triumphalism, Tarzan and Other Influences: Teaching About Africa in the 1990s." Manuscript, Palo Alto, CA: 1993. There are many examples of informed criticisms of the positivistic model of educational planning. See Rolland Paulston, "Mapping Paradigms and Theories in Comparative Education." Paper presented to the Comparative and International Education Society Annual Meeting, Annapolis, MD, March 1992; Hans N. Weiler, "Why Reforms Fail: The Politics of Education in France and the Federal Republic of Germany." *Journal of Curriculum Studies*, 1989; 21: 291–305. For a postmodern analysis with educational references, see Henry Giroux and Peter McLaren, "America 2000 and the Politics of Erasure: Democracy and Cultural Difference Under Siege." *International Journal of Educational Reform*, 1992; 1 (2): 99–100.

2. Chapter 2 in this book offers an analysis of constructivism. We have argued elsewhere that the basis of Habermas' conception of knowledge is a constructivist (i.e., historical and social theory) theory of truth based on the notion of knowledge as a kind of discourse involving a provisional consensus within a scientific community, therefore, based on a principle of fallibilism a la Karl Popper but radicalized in terms of procedural argumentation (Morrow & Torres, 2002: 47).

3. The National Security Strategy of the United States, issued on September 20, 2002 by the Bush administration, has been characterized as neo-imperialist policy by many analysts. See, for instance, the critique of Harvard Paul and Catherine Buttenwieser University Professor Stanley Hoffmann, "The High and the Mighty: Bush's National Security Strategy and the new American hubris." *The American Prospects* http://www.axisofevildoers.com/cache/2003/2003.01.12_1903501512.html.

4. *Humanist militarism* is a euphemism that refers to the US-declared attempt to export democracy by carpet bombing of both civilian populations and what are considered combatant enemy factions.

5. See Carlos Alberto Torres, "Comparative Education: The Dialectics of Globalization and its Discontents in Arnove and Torres." *Comparative Education: The Dialectic of the Global and the Local*. Lanham, MD: Rowman and Littlefield 2007. Pp. 389–403.

6. New Evaluation Committee of the Senate/DEO.

7. Morrow and Torres, *Reading Freire and Habermas*. New York: Teachers College Press, 2002, p. 52.

8. Morrow and Torres, *Op. cit.*, p. 43.

9. I use the term *positivism* to refer to a set of theoretical premises that has informed conventional social science in its attempt to differentiate itself from the humanities, and at the same time, to get the luster of "'scientificity,' drawing on the parallels to the medical sciences, physics, chemistry, etc. A comprehensive metatheoretical analysis of these debates can be found in my book with Raymond Morrow, *Social Theory and Education* (1995). Yet, I should also mention that under other terms and guises, theoretical constructs, such as Rational Choice Theory, and to a lesser extent, Game Theory, to name just two theories with currency in academic settings, may also be criticized along the same lines and in the same spirit as my critique of positivism. Finally, I hope it is clear to the reader that my critique is in no way an attempt to avoid a most important part of our scientific endeavor: to conduct empirical research to know exactly what is going on in reality. Unfortunately, many critical pedagogues have made a habit of writing essays without having gotten their hands wet in the empirical examination of reality. Yet, to conduct empirical research while trying to pretend that ideology doesn't exist, or that values do not intervene at each turn of events, or that we can be completely value-free in the analysis of data, being

politically neutral and scientifically objective are, in their most perverse definitions, simply a ruse or, in a less shrouded expression, a naiveté, which is obviously unacceptable for social scientists.

10. This section summarizes some of the arguments in Chapters 2 and 3, and
draws on my previous work on neoliberalism, structural adjustment, the
neoconservative state, and the World Bank. See for instance, Torres, C. A.
Las secretas aventuras del orden. Estado y educación. Buenos Aires, Argen-
tina: Miño y Dávila Editores, 1996; Pedro Demo, Introduction. In Carlos A.
Torres *Teoría Crítica e Educação.* São Paulo, Brazil: Instituto Paulo Freire &
Cortez Editores, 2003; Torres, C. A. "Structural Adjustment, Teachers, and
State Practices in Education: A Focus on Latin America." In *Educational
Change and Educational Knowledge: Changing Relationships Between the
State, Civil Society and the Educational Community*, T. J. Popkewitz and A.
Kazamias (editors). Albany, NY: State University of New York Press, 1999.

11. Morrow & Torres, 2002: 59.
12. Marcuse, 1941: 252–253.
13. Smith, 1994: 188–189.
14. Carlos Alberto Torres, "Education and the Archeology of Consciousness:
Freire and Hegel." *Educational Theory*, 1994; 44 (4). Pp. 429–445.
15. Marcuse (1966) 1991.
16. Marcuse, 1941: 259.
17. Cited by Marcuse, 1941: 277.
18. Marcuse, 1941: 322.
19. Horkheimer, (1937) 1972a, p. 323.
20. Marcuse, 1941: vii.
21. Max Horkheimer, *Critical Theory: Selected Essays.* New York: Continuum.
1982, p. 232.
21. Morrow & Torres, 2002.
22. Marx, 1935: 356.
23. Ricoeur, 1981.
24. Bowles and Gintis, 1986.
25. Torres, 1995, 1998; Carnoy, 1984.
26. Laclau and Mouffe, 1985; Laclau, 1990.
27. Morrow and Brown, 1994: 11.
28. Kellner, 1989.
29. Kellner, 1989: 7.
30. Kellner , 1989: 7.
31. Rhoads and Rhoades, 2006.
32. Cited in Habermas, 1985: 77.
33. See my arguments in defense of a political sociology of education in Torres,
C. A. "Critical Social Theory and Political Sociology of Education: Arguments." In *Critical Social Theory in Educational Discourse*, T. J. Popkewitz
and L. Fendler (editors). New York: Routledge, 1999.

NOTES TO CHAPTER 7

1. Paper originally prepared for the Fifth International Conference on Transformative Learning. Teachers College, Columbia University, New York,
October 20–22, 2003.
2. A Yugoslavian aphorism cited by Immanuel Wallerstein in "A Left Politics
for the 21st Century? or, Theory and Praxis Once Again." *Democratie*,
Binghamton: Fernand Braudel Center, University of New York, Binghamton, 1999, p. 1.

3. Held, 1991: 9.
4. Luke and Luke, 2000: 287.
5. Urry, 1998.
6. Castells, 1997; Touraine, 1988.
7. Wallerstein, 1979, 1980.
8. Morrow, 2003.
9. In this paper I focus on transformative social justice learning, but I am aware that this construct needs to be enriched reflecting the diversity of oppressive situations.
10. Paulo Freire, *Pedagogy of the Oppressed*. Montevideo, Uruguay: Editorial Tierra Nueva, 1972, p. 19.
11. Paulo Freire, *Pedagogy and Politics*. Los Angeles: Latin American Center, 1998, p. 56.
12. We are thankful to Walter Feinberg for this suggestion in a personal communication to the author.
13. M. P. O'Cadiz and C. A. Torres, "Literacy, Social Movements, and Class Consciousness: Paths from Freire and the São Paulo Experience." *Anthropology and Education Quarterly* 1994; 25 (3); Torres, C. A., *Pedagogia da luta. De la pedagogia do oprimido a la educação publica popular*. São Paulo, Brazil: Cortes Editores and Institute Paulo Freire, 1998; Pilar O'Cadiz, Pía Linquist Wong, and Carlos Alberto Torres. *Democracy and Education. Paulo Freire, Social Movements, and Educational Reform in São Paulo*. Boulder, CO: Westview Press, 1998.
14. Paulo Freire, cited in Moacir Gadotti, *Pedagogía de la Tierra*. Mexico: Siglo XXI, 2002, p. 27.
15. Morris Burman. 1981. *The Enchantment of the World*. Ithaca: Cornell University Press.

NOTES TO CHAPTER 8

1. Armando Alcantara is a professor at the Center for University Studies of the National Autonomous University of Mexico. He received a PhD in education from UCLA.

Bibliography

Abraham, K. C. 1973. Education for revolution: The significance of Paulo Freire's thought. *Religion and Society (Bengala)* 20: 29–37.

Apple, M. 2002. Patriotism, pedagogy, and freedom: On the educational meanings of September 11th. *The Teachers College Record* 104(8): 1760–1772.

Apple, M. 2004. *Ideology and Curriculum*. 3rd ed. New York: Routledge Farmer.

Arnove, R. and Torres, C. A. (eds). 2007. *Comparative Education: The Dialectics of the Global and the Local*. 3rd ed. Lanham, MD: Rowman and Littlefield.

Arroyo, J. n.d. *Paulo Freire: su ideología y su método*, Zaragoza.

Ayres, R. L. 1983. *Banking on the Poor: The World Bank and World Poverty*. Cambridge, MA: MIT Press.

Bandow, D. and Vásquez, I. (eds). 1994. *Perpetuating Poverty. The World Bank, the IMF, and the Developing World*. Washington DC: CATO Institute.

Baran, P. and Sweezy, P. 1966. *Monopoly Capital*. New York: Monthly Review Press.

Bell, L. 2003. *Beyond the Margins. Reflections of a Feminist Philosopher*. Albany, N Y: State University of New York Press.

Berman, M. 1981. *The Reenchantment of the World*. Ithaca, NY: Cornell University Press.

Boron, A. A. 1991. *Estado, Capitalismo y Democracia en América Latina*. Buenos Aires: Ediciones Imago Mundi.

Bourdieu, P. 2001. "O Neoliberalismo é como a sida." Interview by Romain Leick. *Diário de Notícias*, p. 18, 21 July 2001.

Bovard, J. 1994. "The World Bank and the Impoverishment of Nations." In Bandow, D. and Vásquez, I. (eds), *Perpetuating Poverty. The World Bank, the IMF, and the Developing World*. Washington DC: CATO Institute.

Bowels, S. and Gintis, H. 1986. *Democracy and Capitalism: Property, Community, and the Contradictions of Modern Social Thought*. NewYork: Basic Books.

Bresser Pereira, L. C. 1991. "La crisis de América Latin ¿Consenso de Washington o crisis fiscal?" *Pensamiento Iberoamericano* 19:

Bujazan, M., Hare, S. E., La Belle, T. J., and Stafford, L. 1987. International agency assistance to education in Latin America and the Caribbean, 1970–1984: Technical and political decision-making. *Comparative Education* 23(3): 161–170.

Bunch, C. 2001. "Women's Human Rights. The challenges of global feminism and diversity." In Dekoven, M. (ed), *Feminist Locations: Global and Local, Theory and Practice*. New Brunswick, NJ: Rutgers University Press.

Burbach, R. 2001. *Globalization and Postmodern Politics: From Zapatists to High-Tech Robber Barons*. London: Pluto Press.

Burbules, N.C. and Torres, C.A. (eds). 2000. *Globalization and Education: Critical Perspectives*. New York: Routledge.

Carnoy, M. 1984. *The State and Political Theory*. Princeton: Princeton University Press.

Carnoy, M. 1999. *Globalization and Educational Reform: What Planners Need to Know*. Paris: UNESCO/IIEP.

Carnoy, M. 2001. "El impacto de la mundialización en las estrategias de reforma educativa." *Revista de Educación* (número extraordinario): 101–110.

Castells, M. 1997. *The Power of Identity*. Boston, MA: Blackwell.

Cavanagh, J. 2002. *Alternatives to Economic Globalization. A Better World is Possible. A Report of the International Forum on Globalization*. San Francisco: Berrett-Koehler Publisher.

Coleman, J. 1990. *Foundations of Social Theory*. Cambridge, MA: Harvard University Press.

Coraggio, J. L. 1994. "Human Capital: the World Bank's Approach to Education in Latin America." In Cavanagh, J., Wysham, D., and Arruda, M. (eds), *Beyond Bretton Woods: Alternatives to the Global Economic Order*. London: Institute for Policy Studies and Transnational Institute and Pluto Press.

Cronin, C. and de Greiff, P. 2002. "Introduction: Normative Responses to Current Challenges of Global Governance." In Cronin, C. and de Greiff, P. (eds), *Global Justice and Transnational Politics. Essays on the Moral and Political Challenges of Globalization*. Cambridge, MA: The MIT Press.

Culpitt, I. 1992. *Welfare and Citizenship. Beyond the Crisis of the Welfare State?* London: Sage Publications.

De Bray, E. 2003. "The Federal Role in Schools Accountability: Assessing Recent History and the New Law." Voices in Urban Education. Annenberg Institute for School Reform at Brown University, Spring.

Dimitriadis, G. and Carlson, D. (eds). 2003. *Promises to Keep: Cultural Studies, Democratic Education and Public Life*. New York: Routledge.

Fanelli, J.M., Frenkel, R., and Rozenwurcel, G. 1990. "Growth and Structural Reform in Latin America: Where We Stand." Buenos Aires: documento CEDES 67.

Fox, J. A. and, and Brown, L. D. (eds). 2000. *The Struggle for Accountability. The World Bank, NGOs, and Grassroots Movements*. Cambridge, MA: The MIT Press.

Franco, Fausto. 1973. El Hombré. Construccion Progressiva. La tarea educativa de Paulo Freire. Madrid: Marsiega.

Frantzen, D. J. 1990. *Growth and Crisis in Post-War Capitalism*. Hants, England and Vermont, USA: Darmouth Publishing Co, and Gower Publishing Co.

Freire, P. 1970. *Pedagogy of the Oppressed*. Trans. M. B. Ramos. New York: Continuum.

Freire, P. 1971. *Educación como práctica de la libertad*. Montevideo, Uruguay: Ediciones Tierra Nueva.

Freire, P. 1972. La misión educativa de las iglesias en América Latina. *Contacto* IX/5: 32.

Freire, P. 1973. Education, liberation and the church. *Study Encounter* IX/1.

Freire, P. 1998. *Pedagogy and Politics*. Los Angeles: UCLA, Latin American Center.

Freire, P. 1998. *Pedagogy of Freedom: Ethics, Democracy, and Civic Courage*. Lanham, MD: Rowman & Littlefield Publishers, Inc.

Freire, P., Gadotti, M., Saúl, A.M., and Torres, C.A. 1991. *L' Education dans la Ville*. Paris: Païdeia.

Freire, P. and Macedo, D. 1987. *Literacy. Reading the Word and the World*. South Hadley, MA: Bergin & Garvey Publishers.

Friedman, Thomas L. 2005. *The World is Flat: The Globalized World in the Twenty-First Century*. New York and London: Penguin Press Books.

Fuller, B. 1986. *Raising School Quality in Developing Countries: What Investments Boost Learning*. Washington, DC: The World Bank.

Gadotti, M. 1994. *Reading Paulo Freire. His Life and Work*. Albany, NY: State University of New York Press.

Gadotti, M. 2002. Pedagogía de la Tierra, Mexico, Siglo XXI.

Giroux, H.A. 1985. "Introduction" to Paulo Freire, The Politics of Education. Culture, Power and Liberation. South Hadley, MA: Bergin & Garvey Publishers.

Giroux, H.A. and McLaren, P. 1992. America 2000 and the politics of Erasure: Democracy and cultural difference under siege, *International Journal of Educational Reform*, 1(2) 1992, 99–100.

Gutman, A. 1987. Democratic Education. Princeton, NJ: Princeton University Press.

Habermas, J. 1985. "Psychic Thermidor and the Rebirth of Rebellious Subjectivity." In *Habermas and Modernity*, edited by R. J. Bernstein. Cambridge: MIT Press.

Habermas, J. 1975. Legitimation Crisis, ed. and trans. J. Shapiro.Boston. MA: Beacon.

Habermas, J. 1992. Autonomy and Solidarity, London: Verso.

Harriss, J. 2002. Depoliticizing Development. The World Bank and Social Capital. London: Anthem Press-Wimbledom Publishing Company.

Hartsock, N. 1987. "The Feminist Standpoint: Developing the Grounds for a Specifically Feminist Historical Materialism." In Feminism and Methodology, ed. S. Harding.Bloomington, Indiana: University of Indiana Press.

Held, D. (ed). 1991. Political Theory Today. Stanford: Stanford University Press.

Hetzkowitz, H. and Leydesdorff, L. (eds) 1997. Universities and the Global Knowledge Economy. London and Washington: Pinter.

Horkheimer, M. 1937, "Traditional and Critical Theory," reprinted in Critical Theory: Selected Essays, New York, Continuum, 1972.

Ianni. O. 1993. A sociedade global. Rio de Janeiro: Civilização Brasileira.

Ianni, O. 1996. A era do globalismo. Rio de Janeiro: Civilização Brasileira.

Jacoby, R. 1994. The myth of multiculturalism, *New Left Review* 208, 121–126.

Jameson, F. 1999. Postmodernism or the Cultural Logic of Late Capitalism, Durham, NC: Duke University Press.

Kaur, M. 1999. "Globalization and Women: Some Likely Consequences." In Globalization, Culture and Women's Development, ed. R. Mohini Sethi. Jaipur and New Delhi: Rawat Publications.

Kellner, D. 1989. Critical Theory, Marxism, and Modernity. Cambridge and Baltimore: Polity Press and John Hopkins University Press.

Kellner, D. 2003. From 9/11 to Terror War: The Dangers of the Bush Legacy. Lahnman, Maryland, Rowman & Littlefield Publishers.

Kymlicka, W. and Norman, W. 1994/January. Return of the citizen: A survey of recent work on citizenship theory. *Ethics*, 104.

Laclau, E. 1990. New Reflections on the Revolutions of Our Time. London:Verso.

Laclau, E. and Mouffe, C. 1985. Hegemony and Socialist Strategy. London:Verso.

Levin, H. and Belfield, C. 2004. "Vouchers and Public Policy: When Ideology Trumps Evidence." Occasional Paper N° 95 from the National Center for the Study of Privatization in Education, New York: Teachers College-Columbia University.

Lomnitz L. and Melnick, A. 1991. Chile's Middle Class. A Struggle for Survival in the Face of Neoliberalism. Boulder and London: Lynne Rienner Publishers.

Luke, A., and C. Luke. 2000. "A Situated Perspective on Cultural Globalization." In Globalization and Education: Critical Perspectives, ed. N. C. Burbules and C. A. Torres, pp. 275–97. New York: Routledge.

Mander, J. and Goldsmith, E. 1996. The Case Against the Global Economy and for a Turn Toward the Local. San Francisco: Sierra Books.

Marcuse, H. 1941. Reason and Revolution. London: Routledge and Kagan Paul.

Marcuse, H. 1964. *One Dimensional Man*. Boston: Beacon Press.

Marx, Karl. 1935. *Selected Works*. vol. 1, edited by F. Engels, New York: International Publications.

Mazzarol, T. and Soutar, G. N. 2001. The Global Market for Higher Education. Sustainable Competitive Strategies for the New Millennium. Cheltenham, UK.

McCarthy, C. 1998. The Uses of Culture: Education and the Limits of Ethnic Affiliations. New York: Routledge.

McLaren, P. and Leonard, P. (eds) 1993. Paulo Freire. A Critical Encounter. London and New York: Routledge.

Morales-Gómez, D.A. and Torres, C.A. 1990. The State, Corporatist Politics, and Educational Policy-Making in Mexico (1970–1988). New York: Praeger.

Morales-Gómez, D.A. and Torres, C.A. 1994. "Education for All: Prospects and Implications for Latin America in the 1990s" in Education and Social Change in Latin America, ed. Carlos Aberto Torres. Melbourne: James Nicholas Publisher.

Moran, M. and Wright, M. 1991. The Market and the State: Studies in Interdependence. New York: St. Martin's Press.

Morrow, R., and D. D. Brown 1994. Critical Theory and Methodology. London: Sage.

Morrow, R. and C. A. Torres. 1995. Social Theory and Education. A Critique of Theories of Social and Cultural Reproduction. New York, SUNY Press.

Morrow, R. 2003. Globalization and Culture. Los Angeles, California, manuscript.

Morrow, R. and C. A. Torres. 2002. Reading Freire and Habermas. New York: Teachers College Press-Columbia University.O'Cadiz, M. P., and C. A. Torres. 1994. Literacy, social movements, and class consciousness: Paths from Freire and the São Paulo experience. *Anthropology and Education Quarterly*, 25, (3).

O'Cadiz, P., Wong, P.L., and Torres, C.A. 1998. Education and Democracy:Paulo Freire, Social Movements, and Educational Reform in São Paulo. Bolder, Colorado: Westview Press.

O'Connor, J. 1973. The Fiscal Crisis of the State. New York: St. Martins Press.

Ohmae, K. 1990. The Borderless World: Power and Strategy in the Interlinked World Economy. New York: Harber Business.

Ohmae, K. 1995. The End of the Nation-State: The Rise of Regional Economies. New York: Free Press.

Ovando, C. J. 2004 "Teaching for Social Justice: A Critique of the No Child Left Behind." Paper presented at the California Association of Freirean Educators, Paulo Freire Institute, University of California-Los Angeles, February 28, 2004.

Paul, H. and Buttenwieser, C. n.d. University Professor Stanley Hoffmann, "The High and the Mighty: Bush's National Security Strategy and the New American Hubris." [http://www.reckonings.net/stanley_hoffman.htm]

Paulston, R. 1992. "Mapping Paradigms and Theories in Comparative Education," Paper presented to the Comparative and International Education Society Annual Meeting, Annapolis, MD, March 1992.

Plank, D. 1991 "Three Reports from the World Bank," Pittsburgh, PA, manuscript.

Ramamurti, R. 1988. "Privatization and the Latin American Debt Problem," in Private Sector Solutions to the Latin American Debt Problem, ed. R. Grosse. New Burnswick and London: Transaction Publisher, North-South Center and the University of Miami.

Reich, R. 1988. Education and the New Economy.Washington DC: National Education Association.

Reich, R. 1992. The Works of Nations. Preparing Ourselves for 21st Century Capitalism. New York: Vintage Books.

Reimers, F. 1990. "Educación para todos en América Latina en el Siglo XXI. Los desafios de la estabilización, el ajuste y los mandatos de Jomtien." (Paper presented to the workshop on Poverty, Adjustment, and Infant Survival, organized by UNESCO in Peru, December 3–6, 1990.

Reimers, F. 1994. "Education for All in Latin America in the XXI Century and the Challenges of External Indebtedness,"in Education and Social Change in Latin America, ed. Carlos Alberto Torres. Melbourne: James Nicholas Publisher.

Rhoades, G., and Rhoads, R.A. 2002. The public discourse of U.S. graduate employee unions: Social movement identities, ideologies, and strategies. *The Review of Higher Education*, 26 (2), 163–186.

Rhoads, R. A. 2003. Globalization and resistance in the United States and Mexico: The global Potemkin village. *Higher Education*, 45(2),223–50.

Rhoads, R. and Torres, C.A. (eds) 2006. State, Markets, and the University: The Political Economy of Globalization in the Americas. Stanford, Stanford University Press.

Rhoads, R., Torres, C.A., and Brewster, A. 2003. "Turmoil and Transition in Latin American Higher Education: The Cases of Argentina and Mexico." Paper presented at the Center for the Studies in Higher Education at the University of California, Berkeley, May 5, 2003.

Ricoeur, P. 1981. "Hermeneutics and the human sciences.: In *Hermeneutics and the Human Sciences: Essays on Languages, Action and Interpretation*, ed. John B. Thompson. Cambridge, UK: Cambridge University Press.

Romão, J.E. 2001. Globalización o Planetarización. Las Trampas del Discurso Hegemónico. São Paulo: Instituto Paulo Freire.

Rouse, J. 1987. Knowledge and Power: Toward a Political Philosophy of Science. Ithaca and London: Cornell University Press.

Ruiz Olabuenaga, J., Morales, P., and Marragun, M. 1975. Paulo Freire: concientización y andragogía.Buenos Aires, Argentina.

Saltzman, C. 2001. "The Many Faces of Activism." In Feminist Locations:Global and Local, Theory and Practice, ed. Marianne Dekoven. New Brunswick, Rutgers University Press.

Samoff, J. 1990 "More, Less, None? Human Resource Development: Responses to Economic Constraint." Palo Alto, CA, June 1990, mimeograph.

Samoff, J. 1991. "Chaos and Uncertainty in Development," paper prepared for the XV World Congress of the International Political Science Association, Buenos Aires, Argentina, July 21–25, 1991.

Samoff, J. 1992. "From Lighting a Torch on Kilimanjaro to Surviving in a Shantytown: Education and Financial Crisis in Tanzania," case study presented to the UNESCO-International Labor Organization Commission on Austerity, Adjustment and Human Resources.

Samoff, J. 1993. "Triumphalism, Tarzan and Other Influences: Teaching About Africa in the 1990s," Palo Alto, CA: manuscript.

San Juan Jr., E. 2002. Racism and Cultural Studies:Critiques of Multiculturalist Ideology and the Politics of Difference. Durham and London, Duke University Press.

Sanders, T.G. 1968. The Paulo Freire method:Literacy training and conscientization, American Universities Field Staff, Report West Coast South America XV/1 (1968):18.

Saravia, N.G. and Miranda, J.F. 2004/August.Plumbing the brain drain. *Bulletin of the World Health Organization*, 82 (8).

Shor, I. and Freire, P. 1987. A Pedagogy for Liberation. Dialogues on Transforming Education. South Hadley, MA: Bergin & Garvey Publishers.

Sidhu, R. n.d. Selling Futures to Foreign Students: Global Education Markets. University of Queensland, Australia, manuscript.

Slaughter, S. and Leslie, D.L. 1997. Academic Capitalism: Politics, Policies, and the Entrepreneurial University. Baltimore, MD: Johns Hopkins University Press.

Soros, G. 2002. "Against Market Fundamentalism: "The Capitalist Threat" Reconsidered," in Ethics and the Future of Capitalism, eds. L. Zsolnai and W. W. Gasparski. New Brunswick, and London: Transaction Publishers.

Soysal, N. 1994. Limits of Citizenship: Migrants and Postnational Membership in Europe. Chicago, University of Chicago Press.

Sternberg, R.J. 1977. Intelligence, Information Processing, and Analogical Reasoning. Hillsdale, NJ:Lawrence Erlbaum.

Sternberg, R.J. (1985). Beyond IQ. New York: Cambridge University Press.

Sternberg, R.J. 1983. Criteria for intellectual skills training. *Educational Researcher*, 12, 6–12.

Sternberg, R. J. 1997 "Cognitive Conceptions of Expertise." In Expertise in context: Human and Machine, eds. P.J. Feltovich, K. M. Ford, and R. R. Hoffman. Menlo Park, CA: AAAI Press/The MIT Press.

Stiglitz, J. E. 2002. Globalization and its Discontents. New York: W. W. Norton & Company.

Teodoro, A. 2003. "Educational Policies and New Ways of Governance in a Transnationalization Period." In The International Handbook on the Sociology of Education, ed. C. A. Torres and A. Antikainen. Lanham, MD: Rowman and Littlefield.

Torres, C.A. 1976. La dialéctica hegeliana y el pensamiento lógico-estructural de Paulo Freire: SIC 383.

Torres, C.A. (ed) 1978 Leitura crítica de Paulo Freire. São Paulo: Loyola.

Torres, C.A. 1980. Paulo Freire. Educación y Concientización. Salamanca: Ediciones Sigueme.

Torres, C. A. 1990. *Learning the World*. Paulo Freire en conversation with Carlos Alberto Torres, ACCESS Network (Canadian Public Television). Edmunton, Alberta, Canada. October 1990 videotape.

Torres, C.A. 1990. The Politics of Nonformal Education in Latin America. New York: Praeger.

Torres, C.A. 1991. "A Critical Review of Education for All (EFA) Background Documents," Perspectives on Education for All, Ottawa: IDRC-MR295e.

Torres, C.A. 1994. "Paulo Freire as Secretary of Education in the Municipality of São Paulo," Comparative Education Review, 38 (2), May 1994, pp. 181–214

Torres, C.A. 1994. Education and the archeology of consciousness: Freire and Hegel. *Educational Theory*, 44 (4), pp. 429–445.

Torres, C.A. 1995. Estudios Freireanos. Buenos Aires, Argentina: Libros del Quirquincho.

Torres, C. A. 1996. Las secretas aventuras del orden. Estado y educación. Buenos Aires, Argentina: Miño y Dávila Editores.

Torres, C. A. 1998a. Democracy, Education, and Multiculturalism: Dilemmas of Citizenship in a Global World. Lanham, MD: Rowman & Littlefield.

Torres, C. A. 1998b. Pedagogia da luta. De la pedagogia do oprimido a la educação publica popular. São Paulo, Brazil: Cortes Editores and Institute Paulo Freire.

Torres, C.A. 1998c. Education, Power and Personal Biography. New York: Routledge.

Torres, C. A. 1999. "Critical Social Theory and Political Sociology of Education: Arguments." In Critical Social Theory in Educational Discourse, eds.T. J. Popkewitz and L. Fendler. New York: Routledge.

Torres, C. A. 1999. "Structural Adjustment, Teachers, and State Practices in Education: A Focus on Latin America." In Educational Change and Educational Knowledge: Changing Relationships Between the State, Civil Society and the

Educational Community, ed. T. J. Popkewitz and A. Kazamias. Albany, New York: State University of New York Press.

Torres, C.A. 2002. "La Educación del Futuro y los Dilemas de Nuestra Hora," Cuadernos de Educación, Madrid, September 2002.

Torres, C. A. 2002. Globalization, education, and citizenship: Solidarity versus markets? *American Educational Research Journal*, 39(2), 363–378.

Torres, C. A. 2002. The state, privatisation and educational policy: A critique of neo-liberalism in Latin America and some ethical and political implications. *Comparative Education*, 38, (4), 365–385

Torres, C.A. 2003. Globalizations and Education. Presentation at the Meeting of the Fondazione Liberal, Milano, Italy, May 15–17.

Torres, C.A. 2003. Teoría Crítica e Educação: Introduction by Pedro Demo. São Paulo, Instituto Paulo Freire & Cortez Editores.

Torres, C.A. (ed) 2005. La praxis educative y la acción cultural liberadora de Paulo Freire (Valencia, DENES-Instituto Paulo Freire, Edicions del CreC.

Torres, C.A. 2007. "Comparative Education: The Dialectics of Globalization and its Discontents," In Comparative Education: The Dialectic of the Global and the Local, eds. Arnove and Torres. Baltimore, MD: Rowman and Littlefield, Lanhman.

Torres, C. A., and A. Puiggros, (eds) 1996. Education in Latin America: Comparative Perspectives. Boulder, Colorado: Westview Press.

Torres, C. A. and Rhoads, R. 2003. Globalization and Higher Education in the Americas: Theoretical and Political Constructs. Los Angeles, UCLA, manuscript.

Torres, C.A. and Teodoro, A. (eds) 2007. Critique and Utopia. New Developments in the Sociology of Education in the Twenty-First Century, Lahman, Bolder, New York, and Oxford: Rowman and Littlefield.

Touraine, A. 1988. Return of the Actor: Social Theory in Postindustrial Society. Minneapolis, MN: University of Minnesota Press.

Tynjälä, P. 1999. Towards expert knowledge? A comparison between a constructivist and a traditional learning environment in the university. *International Journal of Educational Research*, 31, 355–442.

Urry, J. 1998. "Contemporary Transformations of Time and Space." In The Globalization of Higher Education, ed. P. Scott, 1–17. London: Society for Research into Higher Education and Open University.

Vyas, N. 2002. "Modi for Reforming Madrassas." The Hindu. Online Edition of India's National Newspaper, Friday, June 14, 2002.

Wallerstein, I. 1979. The Capitalist World-Economy. Cambridge: Cambridge University Press.

Wallerstein, I. 1980. The Modern World-System, II: Mercantilism and the Consolidation of the European World-Economy, 1600–1750. New York, Academic Press.

Wallerstein, I. 1999. A Left Politics for the 21st Century? or, Theory and Praxis Once Again. Democratie, Fernand Braudel Center, University of New York, Binghamton.

Weffort, F. 1967. Educacão e política. Reflexões sociológicas sobre una pedagogía da liberdade, introduction to Paulo Freire: Educação como práctica de liberdade, Rio de Janeiro, Paz e Terra.

Weiler, H. 1989. Why reforms fail: The Politics of Education in France and the Federal Republic of Germany, *Journal of Curriculum Studies*, 21.

Went, R. 2000. Globalization: Neoliberal Challenge, Radical Responses London: Pluto Press.

Winerip, M. n.d. What Some Much-Noted Data Really Showed about Vouchers. http://webmail.aol.com/msgview.adp?folder=SU5CTg=&uid=593618

Youngman, F. 1986. Adult Education and Socialist Pedagogy. London: Croom Helm.

Index

Iraq, 26

J
Japan, 60
John Paul II, 19
journey, 65–66
Jung, Carl, 63, 91

K
Kachur, Jerry, 100, 102
Kantian principles, 6, 37, 55, 74, 78
Karp, Stan, 49–50
Kellner, Douglas, 85
Kerry, John, 44, 45
knowledge, 27–30, 35–37, 40–42,
    65–67, 76–79, 87–88, 103
Korea, 60
Krueger, Alan, 19

L
labor, 13, 16, 60–61, 81–82
Latapí, Pablo, 106, 109
Latin America, 19–20, 31–32, 62–64,
    100–109
Lenin, Vladimir, 80
Letters to Cristina, 70
Levin, Hank, 19, 50, 100
Lomnitz, Larissa, 29
love, 6–7, 63, 70, 88, 91, 94
Loyo, Aurora, 100, 102
Lula da Silva, Luiz Inácio, 29

M
Macartism, 75
Makarenko, Anton, 67
Manheim, Karl, 83
Mao Tse Tung, 87
marginality, 89, 92–95
Marx, Karl, 80–83
Marxism, 68, 73, 80–84
mayéutica, 66–67
Malaysia, 23
Marcuse, Herbert, 38, 80–83
McClafferty, Karen, 100
McNamara, Robert, 30
Melnick, Ana, 29
Menchú Tum, Rigoberta, 102
Mexico, 19–20, 60, 61, 99–108
Mitchell, Ted, 100
Mollis, Marcela, 100, 102
Morales Gomez, Daniel, 100
Morrow, Raymond, 84–85, 90, 99
Mozambique, 34
Muñoz, Humberto, 108

Muñoz Izquierdo, Carlos, 106
Murdoch, Rupert, x

N
Nagao, Akio, 102
nation-state, 14, 21, 48, 55–58, 61, 77,
    89
news, ix, 19
neocolonialism, 34–35
neoconservatism, 1, 30–31, 43, 74–75,
    86
neoliberal globalization, *see globalization*
neoliberalism, aspects of, 1, 14, 29,
    as "common sense", 74, com-
    pared to liberalism, 43, expert
    knowledge and, 28, govern-
    ments, 29, in drivers seat, 43, in
    Latin America, 29, 31, market
    and, 31, NCLB and, 52, oppo-
    sition to, 4, 74, policy tools
    of, 30
Neo-Marxism, 35, 55, 82–84, 101
neutrality, 47, 64, 76
New Left, 33, 64, 69
No Child Left Behind, 43–52

O
O'Cadiz, Pilar, 100, 105
O'Connor, James, 14
OECD, 15–16
Offe, Claus, 83
Ohmae, Keinichi, 14
oppression, 6, 63, 66, 71–73, 91–94
Orfield, Gary, 17
Ovando, Carlos, 49–50

P
Pakistan, 23
Patriot Act, 26
patriotism, 22–23, 26, 75
Paulo Freire Institute, 25, 49, 104
Pax Americana, 74–75
*Pedagogy in Process: The Letters to
    Guinea-Bissau*, 63
Pedagogy of Autonomy, 101
Pedagogy of Hope, 70
Pedagogy of the Oppressed, 3, 63, 91–92,
    101, 102, 104
people of color, 17, 13, 19, 51, 82
Pérez Esquivel, Adolfo, 102
Pescador, José Angel, 100
Peterson, Paul E, 18
Phenomenology, 68
planetary consciousness, 6